ARE YOU READY FOR YOUR INSPECTION?

3RD EDITION

VANESSA DOOLEY

Copyright © 2022 Vanessa Dooley
All rights reserved.
ISBN:
ISBN-13

CONTENTS

Acknowledgments	vii
1. The Why!	1
2. The Judgements	9
3. What Is The Point Of Self-Evaluation?	39
4. The Call	48
5. The Learning Walk	59
6. Quality Of Education	67
7. Behaviour And Attitudes	127
8. Personal Development	144
9. Leadership and Management	162
10. So Now What	203
11. Testimonials	205
12. Final Words	212

DEDICATION

This is the third edition of this book. Like with everything in our sector, reflection is key. This book is dedicated to all those people who are aiming to make a difference in children's lives. And to all the settings that have stayed open and worked their socks off to maintain a sense of normality for children throughout the pandemic.

This book is for the Early Years Sector, all the practitioners, managers, and owners who carried on when the rest of the world stopped. Whatever you are doing, keep adding the **IMPACT**.

You are **Early Years Sticks of Rock!** *I couldn't be more proud to work alongside you, raising the game even when the chips were down.*

I hope that the revised edition of this book will prove invaluable and provide you with further guidance to improve outcomes for children and add IMPACT.

Remember we are all #inittogether.

ACKNOWLEDGMENTS

UPDATE:

The acknowledgements I made in the first two editions of this book are as relevant today as they were when I first put pen to paper. However, as I sit down and write this I want more than anything to thank you the reader. The reader who has taken time out of their day to read this book. The reader who has consistently shown up to watch my Facebook Lives. The reader who has been listening to our Are You Ready for Your Inspection? podcast. The reader who opens our emails and even responds. I read every one of them.

You, the reader, give me fire in my belly to carry on. And believe you me, it has been tricky. As I am writing this, I have taken myself away from the Jigsaw Hub, my gorgeous home and family, to have some space to clear my head and concentrate on this book. I've left it too long since updating it last, but I wanted to see how everyone is feeling and know that you are feeling the same way I am.

So, thank you from me to you for fuelling my passion in Early Years.

Secondly, I have to start by thanking Mr D, my husband, for being my first friendly critic who has always challenged me to ask myself the question, WHY? Over the past eight years, and through the whole book-writing process, you have always been there to encourage me and be my rock. My world is a better place with you in it. (Slush moment over!)

My children, Emily and Harry, I need you to know how proud I am of what you have achieved. The journey we have travelled over the past eleven years has shown you are resilient, strong and beautiful people. You can achieve anything once you put your mind to it.

Go and make a difference.

My parents, aka Terry and Joan... well, what can I say. You are my world and I love you both dearly. The role of daughter to parent is continuously evolving in our relationship, but this comes with laughter and tears. Simply, thank you for making me who I am!

And last but not least to the cheerleaders in my life who are constantly putting my crown back on straight when crooked, without me knowing. Emma Smith (Topanga)... You are just the best. And as time moves on so does the amount of support I receive. From old friends to new friends in the IMPACT pods... which you so aptly called yourself; you keep me on track and I am honoured to have you in my life.

To the team in the Jigsaw Hub that started out as one, the lovely Kate, and grew to include Lucy and Anthony who keeps us both calm. As well as these lovely people I couldn't do my job without the Jigsaw Field Team who visit settings as well as me; Hannah and Lorraine, thank you for your support.

Everyone needs a cheerleader in their life and over the last couple of years, the online space has become the platform to find those friends. But alongside that space not only comes online friendships but face to face ones too, and that person is Sue Tydd. Even though some would say we are not true friends, we really are! Who else sees my warts and all and listens to me when the going gets tough?

1
THE WHY!

I have often wondered why people would want to write books, and here I am actually going ahead not only writing one, but also writing its second and third edition. With the ever-changing world we live in, we have to keep up-to-date with all that is happening. And believe you me the world is changing as we speak.

Let me first say if you have got this far that I want to clarify some things for you. Yes, I have left most of the second edition in this book, the reason being, what is the point of changing it if it is still relevant. Am I right?

However, I have added more golden nuggets of information to help you prepare for your inspection. Since Ofsted are now back out inspecting, and have been for the past six months (as I am writing this), we are seeing the shift change and the inspections are becoming more stressful. This is why I want this book to help you shine on the day as well as look at what you do well and what you need to improve on.

So, I never thought I would have written a book and have to say this is one of the proudest moments of my life. Especially when it got to number 1 in 6 categories as well as number 22 out of the entire book section on Amazon! That is something to be proud of and it's not something that sits comfortably with me... but I've said it out loud now.

I would often be in awe of authors for retaining so much information in their heads and wanting to get it out onto paper to share with others. As well as the fact they were so knowledgeable and brainy to be classified as authors.

Yes, they are good at what they write.

But this attribute alone does not make people brainy; it does, however, showcase their talent in wanting to share what they know.

So, during my time as a trainer and consultant, whenever the discussion came about as to why do I not write a book, my first thoughts were a combination of the following:

- I do not have that much information in my head to write about!
- Do I have the knowledge in the first place?
- Another one was... Who, me? The person who left school with only CSEs... Yes, I am that old!

But then, when I started putting pen to paper, I realised, for me, it was more of a mind explosion on paper. So much so, that I could not seem to stop.

As a friend once said to me... it is like your brain dumps all that you know on paper.

So true!

Once the brain dump exploded, I needed to first lay out and then compile these minuscule pieces of information. Creating massive pieces of knowledge that would hopefully be of some use and add some IMPACT.

I became excited and thought, WOW! All this information was actually inside my head, it needed to be released... not only for my sake but also for others.

This could be of help to people who so often find themselves in situations that have troubled me so many times.

So now is the time for me to share what I know, and from both sides of the coin, so to speak.

Background

I have always been into Early Years. As a matter of fact, my passion is Early Years. When Princess Diana announced her engagement to Prince Charles, that's when I knew I wanted to be a nanny. It was a craze... not sure why but I wanted to follow in her footsteps. It was indeed massive for me to realise that there was a job out there that would fit perfectly into my whole perception of meaningful existence. Today, I think I was very lucky to have that thought process so early on. I mean, how many teenagers know what they want to do with their lives when they are at school and take that on earnestly?

The thought of achieving the coveted NNEB was beyond my belief, beyond anything I thought I could achieve in my lifetime. Yet, with the help of amazing friends, a supportive husband, children and parents, and the most inspiring Mrs Espezel (yes, we used to call them Mrs in those days), I was able to achieve my ultimate goal.

To cut a long story short, this is where I am today.

I have managed several nurseries and even group-managed six at one time; all achieving the grand outstanding grade. It was a huge role for me and one I am so proud of, as it helped me get to where I am today. Without the support of the company owners, I would never have achieved my degree or EYPS, yet another wow moment. Sporting that gown and making my parents *and* children proud was just an extraordinarily awesome day.

Leaving the group of nurseries was the hardest thing I've ever had to do, but thinking back to that time now, it was the making of the real me. I've always been determined and passionate. I've had this keen desire to see what else was out there, and so I dipped my toes into new pastures. I worked my way up as an assessor, internal verifier, lecturer, course director for level 2 and 3 as well as the Foundation Degree, in addition to being an Early Years inspector.

Little old me, an inspector! And I still pinch myself, thinking how on earth did I get that far? But with the most amazing support from my shadow inspector, who I still meet for coffee and cake, I did manage to achieve the pinnacle of my career.

But then things started to change… throughout my time inspecting, I was always asking questions about training such as how settings accessed it and how they self-evaluated their practice. In fact, I remember the staff being petrified when I would turn up to inspect, even though throughout the initial phone call, I would try to make them feel at ease. I vividly remembered what it was like… those sick feelings of what I am going to be asked? How will the staff react to the observations? What if we have got something wrong? And so on.

One thing I do want to say at this stage is that before an inspection my husband ALWAYS wished me good luck before I left the house. Why? You would ask. Because, as an inspector, you are entering someone else's domain, home, pride and joy; and you are on your own. Consider the vulnerability in this scenario.

So anyway, throughout the inspections, I realised that I needed to get the best out of the settings and their staff. Inevitably, the only way to do that was for them to feel confident in their own setting and shine... yes... SHINE.

This is your one and only chance to show how good you really are. This is your chance to ensure all the needs of your children, staff and your own self are being met, while also ascertaining the level of impact you are making.

The word IMPACT will be a common theme in this book alongside SO WHAT? And it could not have come at a better time with the new Education Inspection Framework adding the words INTENT, IMPLEMENTATION, and IMPACT in the heading of Quality of Education. It is almost like someone 'up there' was looking down on me when I originally wrote this book, as well as creating our #JustQuality ADDING IMPACT accreditation. What perfect timing!

If you believe in those types of things... I do and thank you Nan x

During my inspector training, the senior inspector drilled into us the words, SO WHAT? particularly when we were writing our report. And I have incorporated the use of these throughout my consultancy and training, in fact so much so, that I am now seeing those words being used in settings when I revisit them.

So, this is where this book comes into its own. I wanted to share with you the fundamentals of inspection, help you feel empowered and get prepared for your inspection.

There is no manual on this critical event. (This is what I wrote in the last editions, which makes me smile and I want to leave it in here... as there is a manual.) Our Are you ready for Your Inspection Manual that we have created, has everything I speak about in this book in a format that you can copy for yourself. It has ideas and golden nuggets of information that I feel will get you prepared; if this is something you are interested in then check it out on our website. This is not a sales pitch, but have a sneaky peek! Some owners and managers have even said it is their Early Years bible and I'll take that.

Here is the link and you will be able to see all the reviews too:

www.jigsawearlyyearsconsultancy.com/product/are-you-ready-for-your-inspection-manual/

So, there are books that talk about outstanding practice, there are books that talk about being the leader in an Early Years setting, there are even audit books that are great if you like a tick list and who doesn't in Early Years? But throughout my research, there has never been an instruction guide, a how-to book, a manual on *how to prepare for your inspection*.

I am not prescribing who this book is aimed at as in my eyes it is aimed at everyone who works in an Early Years setting from apprentices, practitioners, managers and owners, whether you are a preschool, day nursery or even a childminder working on your own. You still need to be prepared. FACT.

If you are a new manager, this will help to take you through the process from the start to the never-ending finish line. If you are an experienced manager, this book will help remind you of those everyday actions you need to do but do not necessarily have the time for. If you are working in an Early Years setting or as a childminder this book is a great tool to guide you on what to expect during your inspection.

This book will hand-hold you through the journey of the entire process making sure that you are going to shine, you are going to be confident, and you are going to show how you add impact.

During market research, I have always asked this: What is it that you truly want? I've listened, and I've taken this away and put together this golden nugget so that you are prepared for your inspection.

There will be some useful tips, some good practice guides, and some guidance to take you forward in your mission to be prepared.

Throughout the many inspections I have done with Tribal, Ofsted, or as part of Jigsaw Early Years Consultancy Quality Improvement Audits, (you may know them as Mock inspections but I do not like that name as it has a negative connotation), I have always seen how nervous staff are when inspectors walk in through the door. I too have been on that end of the spectrum. Through managing many nurseries and group-managing six at a time, I used to dread the knock at the door… the showing of the badge and announcement of the word - Ofsted. These were the days of unannounced visits. I do wish we still had those as we should be adding impact every day, and not just for the inspection day. This subject involves a huge debate.

The journey through opening your setting, preparing for your inspection and actually enjoying the inspection itself is no mean feat - trust me on this. My thoughts are impelling me to write down everything I know, to share all my insight. The motto '*sharing is caring*' is not only highlighted but also exemplified in this case. You need to shine for others. This book will help you get fully prepared for that day by being consistently outstanding, every single day.

You can make this happen. Let me help you make it happen.

Enjoy the journey and, equally importantly, enjoy the process.

Remember, not everyone will understand your journey.

THAT'S FINE.

It's not their journey.

It's yours!

And what a journey it has been.

2

THE JUDGEMENTS

The recently instated Education Inspection Framework was effective from September 2019. It sets out the principles that apply to inspection, and the main judgements that inspectors make when carrying out inspections of maintained schools, academies, non-association independent schools, further education, skills providers and registered Early Years settings in England.

It might be important to note that we are only focusing on the Early Years within this book. However, the headings are all identical, and correspondingly, the process will be similar.

The Early Years Education Inspection Framework provides a powerful and important tool for parents, as well as carers, regarding the quality of education, training and care. Your inspection results will help parents make informed choices as to whether their child should attend your setting.

If you were inspected between July 2013 and July 2016, you are now back 'in the pot' and need to be prepared anew for the call. Evidently, it has become harder to achieve *outstanding*, and maintain that grading, with the goalposts being moved in the new inspection framework. However, since writing this paragraph, Ofsted are still trying to catch up with their inspections. Over the past 18 months as I am writing this, freelance inspectors have had to find new jobs as they have lost all that they were doing, so there is a massive recruitment drive at present to get more inspectors.

But with this, it means that inspections for settings that have been previously graded good and outstanding, can now be over six to seven years before they get visited again. This is causing so much stress within the sector and I have been seeing many grades being lowered due to the fact that they have not been monitored as there has not been a chance.

However, if we consistently strive and work towards it on a day-to-day basis, it will be easier to achieve the grading you desire on the inspection day.

Firstly, let us reiterate, we know that each child is unique. This is very true to your own setting and also to your own inspection. Your inspector will use the Inspection Handbook to judge your setting several times throughout the day and evaluate your practice.

I want to add this paragraph in here. So, when I first wrote this book, the first edition, I gave a colleague who was an Early Years inspector, the first chapter to read. I wrote this...

Every child is unique.

Every setting is unique.

Every inspector is unique.

The comment that came back to me was, "Vanessa, you cannot write that." My response was, "But it's true."

But I did take it out. I am feeling particularly brave as I am sat here writing the third edition. Big girl's pants are on and it is going in!

I hear so many stories about how inspectors are not consistent.

I hear so many stories of inspectors being rude.

But I also hear stories of how amazing they are too!

We do have to remember if we are doing what we are supposed to be doing, then the inspection should go swimmingly well.

Use this opportunity to showcase your own ethos and tone without any inhibition. With a continuous, all-out approach, you will be able to maintain your passion to ensure that children are achieving highly. So, when I see on social media comments like, 'I've had the call, THEY are coming tomorrow, what do I need to do?' it scares me! People write different things ranging from, 'My inspector looked at this' to, 'Mine didn't, they only wanted to see this'.

Believe you me, your inspector will only follow the guidance, which is the Inspection Handbook, and I cannot emphasise this enough. Your inspector will ask if you have read the handbook and where you would grade yourself using the grade descriptors. As such, against this backdrop, this book will help bring about clarity of the handbook.

Within the Education Inspection Framework, all areas are covered under the following new headings:

- Overall Effectiveness

- The Quality of Education
- Behaviour and Attitudes
- Personal Development
- Leadership and Management

The four judgements remain the same within the Education Inspection Framework:

GRADE 1 ~ OUTSTANDING

GRADE 2 ~ GOOD

GRADE 3 ~ REQUIRES IMPROVEMENT

GRADE 4 ~ INADEQUATE

Your inspector will make use of their professional judgements using the Early Years Inspection Handbook to clarify, and use the grade descriptors to give you a grade at the end of your inspection.

They will also look at your setting, to assess and see what it would be like for a child in your care, with the potential impact on the children's learning and development.

Outstanding

If you are judged good or outstanding, your next inspection will be within the next cycle, unless you have a serious complaint that needs to be investigated and could trigger an unannounced inspection. In this scenario, good to outstanding settings next inspections could take anywhere between three to four years.

According to the new EIF (2019), *'In order to reach this standard, inspectors will determine whether the Early Years provision meets **all** the criteria set out under good; for that judgement and does so securely and consistently.'*

So, this means that you cannot get some aspects of the judgements in some areas - it has to be all of them. This also applies for the criteria under the outstanding judgement which you will have to meet. So, to reinforce, to achieve an outstanding grade you need to achieve ALL of the good statements as well as the outstanding judgements.

With an outstanding grade, there will be no recommendations.

Good or Requires Improvement

These judgements will follow the best fit and your inspector will consider whether the overall quality of your setting is aligned with the descriptors defined in the handbook.

For requires improvement you will be inspected within the same year.

Inadequate

You'll be inspected again within the next six months.

You'll be told what you must do to remain registered, and the date by which it must be done. In addition, your local authority will be informed, which may affect your eligibility for funding. Hence, it is critically important to get your inspection right.

You are likely to be inadequate if your safeguarding is ineffective; or, any one of the judgements is inadequate; or, you are in breach of any of the EYFS requirements, and this will impact the children's safety or well-being or if the setting has two previous requires improvements judgements and is still not good.

Inadequate with enforcement

You'll be monitored by an inspector. They'll visit you to check how you're progressing against the areas you were told needed improvement.

Ofsted may take further action if there's no improvement.

If you have two inspections in a row where you're judged as *inadequate*, Ofsted can cancel your registration.

So, imagine how hard it is to get *outstanding* and this is the pinnacle of any Early Years setting.

So, what is it that makes you an *outstanding* setting?

In all fairness, this question is debatable. However, the Inspection Handbook enables you to use this as an audit tool in order to evaluate your own setting. This is highly recommended.

It is so hard to explain what *outstanding* entails whilst respecting brevity. So, let us start with the facts.

How do we ascertain what *outstanding* is and, more importantly, how do we ensure our setting reflects this not only on the inspection day but in everyday practice?

I could go on forever, describing what I think it is... but it may well be different from your perception.

I asked this question on social media and not surprisingly, the responses were extremely diverse.

Here are a few examples:

'Children who are loved and nurtured by every practitioner - practitioners who KNOW their idiosyncrasies and bring out the 'best' in them...'

Mine Conkbayir, author and consultant on Applying Neuroscience to Early Intervention

'That all the hard work and planning I put into running a safe, warm, and nurturing learning environment for the little ones to flourish and fulfil their individual potential has been recognised.'

Jenny Kruk-Strzelecki, Childminder

'Engaged children, staff who have the same vision and expectations, reflective practitioners with evidence of reflections, safeguarding as priority with very knowledgeable staff in this area, supportive community for everyone not just children but staff, management, etc. There probably is lots more, but that is some of what I feel it is.'

Carey West, Merton Preschool

As evident from these responses, we all perceive it differently. And, it indeed is.

It is substantially different in every practice. So, how can we show this uniqueness on the day of the inspection? My thoughts are that you can only really show what it is if you are practising it consistently every day. This is a FACT.

You cannot just turn up, become *outstanding* one fine day and demonstrate your ability to do that consistently to the inspector. The question to ask yourself is can we be outstanding every day? I know I certainly can't! But we have to have a good idea of what it looks like, and your inspector will want to see credible evidence of how you've achieved this uniqueness and distinctiveness. Equally important, they will be interested to ascertain how you intend to maintain this for the foreseeable future. The art of evaluating your setting.

No matter how much you think you do not want *outstanding*, and a *good* would suffice, we all know in our hearts that we're ever so anxious to hear those three magical words during the inspection day…

'You are outstanding.'

However, it is often heard from practitioners that they do not want to get *outstanding*. This is because it is extremely challenging to maintain this grading. At the risk of sounding repetitive: If we ensure achieving an *outstanding* practice every day, it would become like second nature and, thus, be much easier to maintain.

Another FACT that must be remembered.

There are many words when writing an inspection report to describe examples of *outstanding* practice... words such as exceptional leadership, inspiring activities that ignite curiosity, highly reflective - to name a few.

But how do we show this in our everyday practice?

To achieve outstanding, you have to ensure you illustrate and include everything that will help you become outstanding in your everyday practice. There is no point just doing it one day and not on the next. This is not how it works.

Children immediately notice the difference and realise that you are doing things differently when the inspector arrives.

I can give you an example of this. I remember one inspection where a practitioner was taking items out of a carrier bag that she had just bought for the day. She wanted to ensure her Easter activities were the most amazing activities ever.

This was not the usual scenario with her.

The children soon realised that they were given an activity, which they had not done before. They actually did not know what to do. They waited eagerly for instructions to be handed over by the practitioner. They were handed pre-cut templates and were asked to stick items around the edges. There was no discussion about the purpose of the activity. And, there was no questioning to ignite their learning from the practitioner either.

Children did not know how to use the glue stick; they were looking at it in a perplexed manner as though they had not seen one before. They were given one pair of scissors to share between three children; however, as the objects were new, they soon began arguing. The practitioner did not interject or explain to the children about the need to share. This soon inflamed into a heated exchange amongst the children and they begin to shed tears. Clearly, the behaviour was not managed effectively and children did not know of any boundaries.

That is not something you want to show on the day of inspection.

Needless to say, the *outstanding* grade in such cases moves further away.

So, my advice is to start thinking about your end game right away and you will be able to shine on the day. After reading this chapter, write down five points, defining what you need to do in order to make an outstanding environment possible. Let this be your pledge to yourself. If we write things down, they become a reality.

So, how are you going to get this grade?

This is where this book comes to your help.

Defining Outstanding

The extensive task of defining *outstanding* would take up a whole book, which is not my intention.

The chapter aims to explicate the fact that *outstanding* means something different to different practitioners, depending on their own perceptions and feelings at any given point in time.

To achieve an *outstanding* grade, you need to have highly effective staff, in fact, a group that is singing from your own hymn sheet. Every practitioner needs to be providing the necessary tools and ensuring they all meet the unique, innate needs of each child. Your staff need to be passionate and committed to their roles within the team and have a sound understanding of the children's developmental needs. This is so important and often missed.

Over the past 18 months (remember I am writing this in October 2021), the Early Years sector has been struggling. Finding the right team members for our settings is now turning into finding any team members for our settings. We are feeling the pinch of not having enough staff to maintain ratios, which is what we need to do. We are feeling the anxiety of having staff who do not want to be in our sector. We are struggling with not being able to pay our staff the wages they deserve. Early Years is struggling. And I wish I could see the light at the end of the tunnel and wave my magic wand and help you all out. I so wish I could. But all I can do is listen and try to give you some pointers to make your life easier.

So, let's get started and think.

Many years ago, when I struggled to achieve my NNEB, our setting's 'Bible' was Mary Sheridan. This gave us the framework for all child development levels and milestones from birth to five years of age. We knew it backwards, left, right, and centre. Can you honestly say all your staff know your ethos?

It is all about the staff

With my background and experience as a lecturer, I have seen students attend because they have to, not because they want to. This often makes me wonder: Where has the passion for students to *want to* learn more about children's development disappeared? I know through the many Jigsaw Quality Improvement Audits, which the Early Years Consultancy has attended, that recruitment is a challenge at the moment and we end up employing staff only to ensure ratios.

Why is hiring reduced to just another tick box exercise?

During my time as an inspector and a consultant, it became increasingly clear that we are using online assessments to inform us of where children currently are in their developmental stage and not taking much notice of whether this is right. So, my first recommendation would be to ensure that all practitioners in your setting have an in-depth understanding of child development. What do your staff know about the Early Years Foundation Stage? Do you or your staff know about the ages and stages of development? Certainly, the inspector would want to see that you are knowledgeable in this area. It is the responsibility of the leader or manager to make sure that all standards are not only met but also kept high – an aspect that should be tangible and visible throughout the day. They need to make sure all of their team are on board and able to contribute confidently during the day of the inspection.

At the same time, practitioners need to be passionate and committed to their roles and have a firm understanding of the children's needs. I repeat this point so that you can reflect on this and take a look at the staff within your setting or yourself as a childminder, before deciphering what they know about the stage of development of a particular child - and how they are going to achieve their next steps.

Remember you are only as strong as your weakest link!

It is all about the staff!

Audit and monitoring

Your staff are the pinnacle to achieving *outstanding;* let there be no doubt about it. They are the significant others who are shepherding children in their journey of learning and development and the onus is on you as the manager, to ensure that this is indeed happening.

But how can you guarantee they are?

As well as having outstanding staff, you will need to show that you are secure in your EYFS requirements through ably demonstrating your willingness to work above and beyond the expectations. You will now need to know your curriculum. We will discuss this later on in the book.

You will need to show that children are making consistent and significant progress in all areas. If not, why not and how are you ensuring this is being monitored?

It is the managers'/providers' responsibility to ensure that all the welfare requirements are being adequately met. To that end, use the Statutory Framework for the Early Years Foundation Stage (2017) as an audit tool in order to look at what you are doing under each heading and how this impacts the children within your setting.

If you are a preschool, you may be the manager in place, but you may also be run by a committee.

Let me just clarify this: If you are a committee-run preschool, your committee has a major responsibility on its shoulders.

I have been to so many inspections where the preschools are working really hard to demonstrate the impact and ensure that children's needs are being met, but this comes to a standstill when the committee has failed to be compliant in their roles.

This can include not informing Ofsted about new committee members to ensuring their DBS are up to date, or not following the correct procedures for the managers' induction. I just cannot emphasise this point enough: The committee members have got to be fully involved and participative within their setting. They are classified as providers and, therefore, need to take on the complete responsibility of the setting. So, if you are a committee-run setting, take a step back and ask yourself this question.

Is the committee fully aware of their duties within their roles?

In case the answer is no, this is the chance to make those changes and arrange a meeting in order to discuss how important this is to the setting and children.

What is the point?

Are you reading this and already thinking, 'Wow, there is too much to know, digest and amend in my setting!'

Do you ever get those days where you think what is the whole point?

When was the last time you took a step back and thought – WOW, today was amazing?

Getting my point? Food for thought, for sure!

Throughout my inspection and consultancy, I have been so thrilled to see many settings accomplish for themselves an *outstanding* rating.

This was their ultimate goal.

Poignantly, the next part of achieving outstanding is to maintain it. So surely, wouldn't it be easier if this was an everyday process and therefore easier to maintain this mindset and mechanism?

So, what do you need to become *outstanding*?

It all starts with a vision

Does your setting have a vision?

This vision not only has to be led by an excellent leader; it also needs to be carried forward by a team that is on board and yes, all the way.

I was once taught by an inspiring leader of a group of nurseries, 'Speed of the leader, Speed of the team'.

I cannot stress this enough.

We all have an idea of where we want to go and the ultimate goal is to achieve that cherished judgement of *outstanding*.

"Your vision will become clear only when you can look into your own heart. Who looks outside, dreams; who looks inside, awakes."

Carl Jung

Starting with your vision,

- Have you ever asked your staff what it is?
- Do your staff team know and live your ethos?
- Why not take this time to ask the question?

'The highly skilled and passionate management team leads the provision with enthusiasm and dedication. Its vision for excellence is reflected in the highly focused and inspirational staff team. Together they strive to provide a first-rate service for children and their families'

Starfish Day Nursery, Oldham

If your staff are not aligned with your mission and vision, then this, in fact, will be potentially the first point of call. Start off with a staff meeting and ask them, what they think it is. It's interesting to hear what their views are, and how good would it be if they came up with an idea that can help in promoting that vision?

A staff meeting could be a way of showing staff that you are prepared to listen, which is so important. I have been to settings where practitioners have said they are not listened to. Showing your team that you have the ability to respect and assimilate their views, can have the same positive effect as when we listen to children.

It gives them a feeling of self-worth, a sense of value and the much-needed confidence to share ideas. Once you are on board with your setting's vision, this is where and how the goals are set across the team.

What is your purpose for your setting?

What are you trying to achieve and how are you going to get there? This is a great start for reflecting and evaluating your setting which we will talk about in the next chapter.

Communication

> *"The art of communication is the language of leadership."*
>
> **James Humes**

The art of effective communication - is this an art?

One of the most important themes of any setting is how a leader or manager communicates with his/her team.

Now is the time to reflect. List the various ways in which you communicate with your team.

Once you have documented this, look closely at each method and think about the way this information is received. Put yourselves in their shoes.

Consider: How often do you have staff meetings? Do all staff members attend? Do you invite ALL staff members? If no, why not? Can you imagine what it would be like to not be invited to a meeting? Surely, this does not help the entire staff to feel valued or involved.

What about those who do not attend? How can you ensure the entire team is aware of the meeting agenda and have understood the messages being discussed and relayed?

For example, once I was inspecting a setting and asked a member of staff what they understood about Prevent duty and FGM. The staff member looked at me and said that she was not at the staff meeting when this was being discussed. She then went on to clarify that she does not go to staff meetings as she was 'only covering staff'.

This conversation and her expressions made it abundantly evident to me that she felt undervalued and that she was just there to make sure ratios were being adhered to.

Is that a great start?

Surely, making sure that the entire staff is involved in the day-to-day running of the setting is paramount to achieving an *outstanding* practice.

Think about this. Would we as practitioners not include all children?

I am hoping you are saying no Vanessa, never. Then why do we feel that we do not need to include the entire staff when it comes to communication?

Now, I totally understand that not everybody can attend meetings due to other commitments, but then it's important to have that discussion with them to help them feel involved in being part of the team and the mission and vision at large.

So, the next time you have a meeting, think about all the staff and how you can best communicate with them. Think about the minutes of those meetings. Can they be shared with staff via messenger or WhatsApp, if needed? Make them feel part of the team.

If you are a childminder and have an assistant, this open and participative communication is also the key for your type of setting. How do you ensure they all are working alongside you towards your vision?

You need to show that your staff's views are being listened to and taken on board wherever applicable. This demonstrates a leader as being highly effective - a trait which an *outstanding* judgement stands by.

As part of an effective communication system, we need to have the ability to listen to others before we can get our points of view across. We also must factor in peoples' points of view, successes as well as their apprehensions.

> "The most basic of all human needs is the need to understand and be understood. The best way to understand people is to listen to them."
>
> **Ralph Nichols**

It is interesting as I am re-writing this I have been back out visiting settings with our Quality Improvement Audits since April 2021 and I have noticed that some staff teams are struggling with how to communicate with each other. We have lost the art of interacting with not only ourselves but with children and feel we need to go back to basics. We will never learn anything; children will never learn anything without effective communication. We must get this skill back otherwise children are going to fall behind even further in their communication and language skills.

Having active listening skills within your setting is important to show you are prepared for any change and remain open as well as receptive to new ideas. This, in turn, shows that you are working towards building an *outstanding* setting.

You must be able to demonstrate a coherent vision, determination, and passion for continuous improvement. You also need to be able to consistently reflect and assimilate others' viewpoints, irrespective of how conflicting they are to help improve outcomes for children.

After thinking about the way you communicate with staff, think about how you're going to communicate with parents.

- How do you ensure that all communication with the parents is effective and consistent?
- Do you involve all parents?

We will talk about this further in the chapter on Leadership and Management, but it does give you some food for thought. This is one of the key reporting requirements which is needed to ensure the best outcomes for children.

Focus on the children's needs

As a leader, you must show your level of expertise from the very start. You must inspire hope and always focus on the children's needs. Their needs are at the forefront of your setting, something that must be portrayed and felt throughout your entire team. You need to understand and be honest about your journey and know how to take your team through it. At the same time, you need to be extremely reflective and highly engaging in getting things done to achieve the best possible outcomes for children.

Children in your setting need to continually achieve in their chosen areas of learning. If they are not, you need to assess why not, and demonstrate that you are doing everything possible to address the problematic areas. Notably, *outstanding* does not necessarily mean all children are achieving highly; it's more to do with how you are ensuring their continual learning and development for each one of them is successful. Remember, every child is unique and has individual needs, which you need to identify and support.

Now it is time for you to reflect upon what you do in your own setting. Go to a quiet, secluded place for about 30 minutes and take an honest look at your setting. I can hear you say in your head as if I have 30 spare minutes for this. If you want to improve your setting, then, certainly this is the much-needed time for reflective practice.

Use the following questions to guide you. And work out if your staff team consistently do this, occasionally do this, or rarely do this.

Throughout this book, there will be some documents that you may want so we have created a space on our website where you are able to download these for free! Who says we are not here to help you?

Here is the link.

www.jigsawearlyyearsconsultancy.com/are-you-ready-for-your-inspection-book-downloads/

The password is #AUR3-2022

Reflective Practice Questions

1. Do you and your staff continually listen to the children and take on board their viewpoints, thus enabling them to progress in the areas of learning and development through their own interests?
2. Do you and your staff continually enable children to choose their own activities to inspire and ignite their curiosity?
3. Do your staff members encourage learning in children through the scaffolding of language and questioning?
4. Are children able to make a choice, have a voice and choose what they want to do through the various activities in a day?
5. Do you and your staff enable children to be independent in their personal development skills through a variety of choices and unrestrained freedom?
6. Do you ensure that in your setting all staff members use relevant and up-to-date training to develop children's skills and demonstrate its impact on them?
7. Do you ensure that all children are consistently kept safe through effective risk assessments by ensuring all safeguarding policies are up to date and ALL staff members are aware of the importance of protecting against different types of abuse, radicalisation, and extremism?
8. Are all staff members aware of any children who are becoming *invisible* in the setting and interact with those children?
9. At any point in time, do you find children wandering around the setting looking for things to do?

10. Are British Values consistently being promoted in the setting among the children by instilling an awareness of different cultures and values of other children in the group?
11. Is a partnership with parents continually being supported and do parents have an understanding of where their children are in their areas of learning and development?
12. Do all parents contribute significantly to their children's learning journey? Do you constantly ensure that all parents (depending on their needs) are working in partnership with you?
13. Are all staff members aware that the activities they undertake for the children need to have an impact? If so, what is the impact that they are hoping to achieve through the children's learning? Are they able to evidence this consistently?
14. Are you able to demonstrate that the setting has an ambitious vision?
15. Do all staff members have high expectations about what each child can achieve? Do they ensure the compliance of high standards of care and the delivery of provision for children at all times?
16. Do you ensure that your staff are ready to improve upon their practice so that they are able to deliver on teaching and learning?
17. Do you evaluate the quality of your setting and ensure it is improved through periodic self-evaluation?
18. Are the views of parents, children, and staff taken into account to impact improvements in the setting?
19. Do you lead the setting to sustainable success through effective planning and manage the curriculum

learning programme to ensure a good start for all the children?
20. Are children being prepared for school during the next stage of learning?
21. Do you actively promote equality and diversity and are trained to tackle negativity?
22. Do you make sure that appropriate arrangements are in place to ensure that all children are kept safe from harm, including prevention against radicalisation and extremism?
23. Do you make sure that the training is highly effective and improving rapidly through ongoing professional development?
24. Do you effectively monitor and identify areas where children may be slow to develop the key skills that they are learning?
25. Do you ensure a highly effective partnership with your parents, as well as outside agencies to ensure that the improvement of provision and outcomes for children is maximised at all times?
26. Do you ensure you listen to how the staff feel about the workload and ensure they understand where to go in case needed, at every supervision?
27. Do you ensure there is a highly effective partnership that not only involves your parents but also outside agencies to ensure that the improvement of provision and outcomes for children is maximised at all times?
28. Do you encourage children to regulate their own emotions and help develop their individual ability to manage their own behaviour?
29. Do you ensure all children experience the awe and wonder of the world in which they live, through the seven areas of learning?

30. Do you have an INTENT every day?
31. Do you implement the INTENT every day?
32. Do you evidence the IMPACT of the INTENT every day?
33. Do your staff team know the curriculum they are wanting children to learn?
34. Do you ensure storytime, rhymes and singing are accomplished with excitement and engagement with every child where new words, concepts, and vocabulary are introduced?

The optimal use of questions should give you a good basis to look at your practice and make improvements.

Your practice is unique to you

The unique word again!

To reiterate, your practice is unique to you and you only. Not all approaches or theories are suitable for every setting.

Although having an Ofsted inspection and guidance is highly important for us, they cannot judge us on the way we deliver practice in our setting unless it breaches welfare requirements, and as long as we are able to demonstrate the impact our teaching is having on our children's learning.

We need to show that we are providing a welcoming, nurturing and evolving practice that meets the needs and outcomes of each child walking through our door. We need to grow as a setting and discover what works well for us and our children.

You all know your children better than anyone else does. Remember that.

We have a range of techniques, which are ideal in regards to the learning styles of children, and we need to ensure that this quality is of the highest form.

By meeting all welfare requirements and the statutory framework for the EYFS, you are well on your way to showcasing your setting. Once this has been achieved, you need to look at your practice, in a step-by-step manner, so as to ensure its efficacy for all children and not just the ones who are exceeding.

Through the eyes of a child

Your inspector will want to see what it is like to be a child in your setting. Your report will have a paragraph allocated to this.

Think about putting yourself in a child's body again... can you remember that far back?

What do you remember? I can probably go back to the age of 5 which for me is around 48 years ago!

Some of those memories were not so great and yet some were amazing.

This is what the Education Inspection Framework is all about.

What is it like to be a child in your setting?

From the moment children enter your setting to when they go home.

To when they go home and when they come back to you again.

Throughout this book, we will be asking the question what it is like for a child in your setting and what impact it has on their learning and development? Especially after what we have been going through with Covid-19 Pandemic. What has it been like for a child during that time? What have you done to ensure their emotional well-being is being nurtured?

Once you start to use this formula then you will start creating a setting that excels in what you deliver and is constantly improving and reflecting on your service.

So, let's start at the beginning of the day.

What happens when a child enters your setting?

While you are reading this I am thinking have you started letting parents back into the setting? If not why not?

Have children settled easier and more confidently without their parents bringing them into the room?

Are they greeted by a member of staff?

Are they asked how they are? It does not matter the age of the child for we are starting the way we mean to go on with the art of conversation... and sometimes we lose sight of that.

When greeted what do we do then?

Is your setting set out ready for children to start learning and playing or do we encourage children to choose from the moment they arrive about what they want to play with?

What do you do? And why do you do it that way? What is the impact of this?

Think about this... if you arrived at your hairdressers and they sat you down in the chair and started creating their masterpiece without asking what you would like? How would you feel?

Insecure, worried, scared?

Whereas if they sat you down and asked, what would you like today and listened to your response you would feel valued, and secure that they understood what you were wanting.

This is the same for children.

Encourage children to make those choices, encourage independence and promote self-esteem, self-worth, and confidence, what a way to promote resilience! We will talk about this further in the Personal Development chapter as this has had a huge impact since Covid-19 pandemic.

So, they have started the day with you with good conversation regarding how they are. Think about how you feel when someone asks how you are and listens... this is the same for a child. The feeling of being valued is of high importance and you are on the right path for children to recognise if they are okay or not. Self-regulation is so important in Early Years, and this is extremely important within this framework. So, think about this... How do you encourage children to regulate their emotions and feel okay to say they are not okay?

Again, through the eyes of the child this is priority.

When it comes to nappy changing or toileting what do you feel a child sees, hears, and feels at this transition?

Just picking a baby off the floor while they are in flow of kicking, stretching, and using their gross and fine motor skills without any recognition of what you are doing to them is such a no and something I have seen on many occasions.

Think about what a baby sees and feels... I don't know about you, but my knees do not speak, so how do we communicate with babies... think about eye level, concentration as well as conversation, expression on our faces, the tone in our voices. This is important in a baby's time with you in your setting.

When you are changing a baby's nappy or toileting with a toddler, talk to them, explain what is happening.

Don't just change their nappy without telling them. Ask them. Okay, there may not be an option as they need their nappy changed, however, explain to them why. They may not understand but they need to know why you are doing what you are doing.

Don't just take them to the toilet without explaining to them why you are sitting them on the toilet… think again through the eyes of a child. It is about a culture of consent. You may be reading this now and saying to yourself – "Vanessa, are you joking?" No I am not. Think about it. Through the eyes of the child.

Throughout all my training I have said think about through the eyes of the child and follow a child. Spend that time choosing a child and following them throughout the day. I would like to suggest the first two weeks of when children enter your setting or transition from one room to another who just take a step back and observe. Watch what they see.

Watch how their key person interacts with them.

Watch how other children interact with them.

Watch how parents interact with them.

This is so important and the basis of an outstanding setting when you can recognise and improve on what you are seeing with interactions with children and staff.

'Getting it right first time' was published in July 2013 to help with achieving and maintaining the high-quality provision of Early Years. Even though it is over five years old, it is still used by inspectors. We should be actively promoting this document in our settings to give us a better understanding of how to get it right the first time.

Areas should be outlined to ensure that settings are aware of what is needed to make a setting *good* or *outstanding*. Strong leadership is crucial. It drives up the quality of a setting's work and ensures all children are encouraged to reach their full potential. We will discuss the attributes of strong leaders later in this book.

3
WHAT IS THE POINT OF SELF-EVALUATION?

A few years ago Ofsted decided that the SEF (Self Evaluation Form) did not need to be uploaded to the portal.

In Early Years we thought this meant we did not need to evaluate what we do in our setting. This is not the case and it is a reporting requirement for settings to evaluate their practice.

The Early Years Inspection Handbook for Ofsted registered provision (2019: pg15) states:

'Leaders and managers of settings should have an accurate view of the quality of their provision and know what to improve. They do not need to produce a written self-evaluation but should be prepared to discuss the quality of education and care they provide – and how well they meet the needs of the children – with the inspector. Inspectors will consider how well leaders and managers evaluate their provision and know how they can improve it or maintain its high standards.'

So, think about how you evaluate your practice and if every staff member in your setting is involved. Evaluating does not mean it has to be all positive, it means the necessary action that you undertake to improve and show how you are adding impact in case something did not go so well.

Your inspector will have conversations with you and your team about their own evaluation and observe this during the inspection process. They will check to see how accurate this is and observe how staff are teaching, how children are learning, how they are progressing and how the parents' perspective is taken on board, and the quality of your setting.

Self-evaluation aka self-assessment

Another term for self-evaluation is self-assessment. So, what does this mean?

"Self-evaluation will help you to consider the best way to create, maintain and improve your setting, so that it meets the highest standard and offers the best experience for young children."

(Page 4 of Early Years Self-evaluation Form Guidance, Ofsted)

Early Years practitioners should constantly reflect on the quality of their work. As professionals, and as members of the staff team, which is accountable for the overall Quality of Education, we need to be made accountable for the quality of your work and for the achievements of the children we teach and engage with.

It is even better when we evaluate as a team as this involves groups of our team reflecting on our work together. There are several ways that this can happen:

- Peer on peer observations.
- Commenting on each other's activities and work.
- Using time to think about the impact we have made each day, week, month.
- Evaluating where we see where a child is in their development and how we can improve on this.
- Working together on good quality play experiences which children can use.
- Thinking about courses that need to be attended and why we need to do them.
- Having that open discussion at the end of the day about what went well and what didn't.

Self-evaluation means that we need to look at what we are doing in the present and think about our strengths and weaknesses, and subsequently consider how can we improve on this?

Every day, whether you are an Early Years setting or not, you are evaluating what you are doing and how you would do things differently next time. Consider the scenario when you make your dinner using a recipe. What happens when you serve this at the table and you all begin tasting the meal you have cooked? Do you think it is just fine, or do you often find asking yourself of ways you can make it taste better next time? We reflect on what we could have done better.

Everyone needs to be reflective and evaluate their practice. How else are we going to improve on the way we do things?

Would it be a shocker for you to know that at the end of my inspections, I would often ask the setting under inspection:

How could I improve on the way I inspected?

The look on the managers' faces when being asked that question was sometimes that of pure horror. The question was: Why would you (as an inspector) want to know that?

Here's the thing. Why wouldn't I want to know?

As a lecturer and trainer, we are trained to reflect on every lesson or training. Correspondingly, we should continually ask ourselves what went well and how we can make improvements the next time. If we do not ask ourselves those hard questions, how can we improve?

Ask yourself these questions:

- Can you improve on managing of your setting?
- Can you improve on working in partnership with parents or others?
- Can you improve the quality of education within your setting?
- If yes, how so? Do you ask your staff how you can improve?

Yes, the question is big and complicated but gives a real insight into you as a leader or manager. If you are open to change, then this *is* the way forward. If not, I would suggest you look for another career. Early Years is very reflective, and we need to be constantly doing this.

IMPACT: What does it mean?

So, how do we do this to show IMPACT... there is that word again... maybe I should explain the meaning of that word before moving on any further.

Impact here means to have a strong effect on someone or something. So, what do you do in your setting that has an enduring effect on a child's learning and development?

Examples could be:

The childminder uses photographs of children and their family members on the display board. Children are eager to name and talk about those photographs.

Based on the sentence above, the impact is that the children are able to feel a sense of belonging and self-worth.

Another example:

The staff makes accurate assessments through teaching opportunities on a daily basis. Children are able to choose and talk about the dinosaurs in the sand tray.

The impact of this is the development of children's confidence and speaking skills through their own interests. They engage in questioning-based interaction and use their critical thinking skills to spark awe and wonder of the world.

Back to self-evaluation - whichever setting you are in, whether it is a day nursery, preschool or you are a childminder - we need to do this. Remember, at the beginning of this book I said that you need to shine... now is your chance. Start with your self-evaluation.

Think about how you can show what you do and the improvements you make every day to make sure the children are attaining those high defined outcomes. While Ofsted does say it does not mandate you to get this written, why not kill two birds with one stone and create a document where you can show tangible evidence to parents, visitors, new staff on interviews - as well as your inspector?

Further on within the book, you will be able to read about our #JustQuality ADDING IMPACT Accreditation which we devised to help Early Years settings demonstrate the several ways which can be adopted to achieve this.

Versions of self-evaluation

Throughout my travels, I have seen many versions of self-evaluation and that's where the motto of *'Sharing is caring'* comes into play. As an inspector, I would always ask about the evaluative quality of the settings. This did not necessarily mean the process needed to be written; however, if it was, it did suggest they were making it a point to record and show whatever they needed to do next. This certainly made a positive difference to the inspection process.

When asked the question: 'Do you struggle to self-evaluate and if so, why?' - The answers were very clear.

Time.

I think I am constantly evaluating but the recording I struggle with. I have started jotting scribbled notes in my diary bullet journal style and that works for me. It may make no sense to anyone but me but it beats banging my head filling in a template that bears no resemblance to my normal way of doing things just to please the powers that be.

When Ofsted come they may or may not like my style but I can talk the hind legs off a donkey about why I do what I do and the impact changes have made so hopefully, that will be enough. I am one little me so I can do no more and I'm good with that.

If these are your issues, let's see if we can make this process easier for you.

Tools on how to reflect and evaluate

Be mindful: This is your setting and your time to shine.

During your inspection, you will be slightly stressed and probably very aware of your staff, children, parents and even the inspector on the day. So let us use the self-evaluation to say the following:

What?: So what?

Now what?

Thank you, Driscoll (1994) for providing us with this simple tool of how to reflect and evaluate.

This means (i) looking at what you do, (ii) what was the impact, and (iii) thinking about what you are going to do to change it to improve. My suggestion would be to break the sections into areas where you are being inspected, as this will ensure that you cover each section.

For example:

Another way of evaluating is by using IMPACT sheets. These can be used for every day or every week and placed in a folder where you are able to see how you are improving. Again a download of this has been created and is on our website for you.

Here is the link:

www.jigsawearlyyearsconsultancy.com/are-you-ready-for-your-inspection-book-downloads/

The password is #AUR3-2022

Have you ever felt you wanted to further accentuate the strengths of your setting? So, why not develop a scrapbook idea which makes it possible for each section to be evaluated on a weekly basis?

Divide the scrapbook into the following sections:

- Quality of Education
- Behaviour and Attitudes
- Personal Development
- Leadership and Management

This is an example of how you can evaluate with impact, and please feel free to add more parameters in order to customise it to your setting. For instance, if you are a day nursery, consider giving your settings' rooms their own learning journal to showcase what they do well and the things they can do to ensure children are continually developing.

This would not only help with your whole evaluation process in your setting; it would also give the team a chance to be involved and take autonomy of their room. In turn, this would make sure that all your staff members are on board with the whole process as opposed to leaving this to you as the owner or manager.

See the last chapter for more ideas!

4
THE CALL

The best preparation for good work tomorrow is to do good work today.

Elbert Hubbard

How do you feel when you get the call?

- Anxious
- Scared
- Nervous
- Irritable
- Excited

Why do you think? Is this how you feel? Is it because this is your first inspection, or because you have had a bad experience before? Or does the word 'inspection' make you feel this way.

Regardless, you need to showcase your setting throughout the process. This is your one and only chance to demonstrate the construct of your setting and staff, and the underlying principles to the Ofsted inspector. I cannot stress this enough to you. Every activity from this day has an IMPACT on you, your staff, your setting, your children as well as your parents. Which is why it is so important to think every day is an inspection day!

When will you get that chance again?

Remember, the inspector is a human being too, who has a family at home just like you and me - and is only doing his/her job! They want children to achieve the best outcomes and can only judge you based on the time they are with you.

With that in mind, SMILE, it will and does make the day go better.

So, think about when answering the setting's phone during the day. Is it usually chaotic and the noise is carried through to where you are answering the phone?

Do you ever think, 'I will leave the phone to ring and I am sure they will ring back?' Yes, people usually do. But one word of caution: The inspector will only make three phone calls to try and make contact with you. If you do not answer the phone on each of these three occasions, they are well within their rights to arrive unannounced!

The inspector will usually call the day before around lunch time...yes I know that is your busiest time. We have devised this chapter to make you well prepared and confident when the call is made.

Preparation is key

If you are a childminder, the call will come approximately five days before your inspection. You will be asked your availability for the next five days in case you have Early Years children.

First impressions count, so make sure that whoever answers the telephone knows how to respond to 'That Call.' Do you have a standard way of answering the telephone? Think about how first impressions are made when you do.

The inspector will explain that they are visiting you the next day (or within the next five days if you are a childminder) and inform you about their arrival time. Make sure to ask their name. This is so important as it will set you at ease and this will also set the tone of the inspection.

Typical questions on the call

At this point, you will be asked questions and it would be good to have the information readily available.

Some of the questions will include:

- How many children currently do you have on roll?
- How many children would you have on the day of inspection?
- How many staff do you have working on that day?
- How many children do you have with EAL?
- How many children do you have with additional needs?
- How many two-year-old funded children do you have?
- Do you have any children with EYPP?

Prompt sheet

We have provided you with a prompt sheet, which will ensure that you are thoroughly prepared to answer these questions.

Visit the website and enter the password to get your free pdf download:

www.jigsawearlyyearsconsultancy.com/are-you-ready-for-your-inspection-book-downloads/

The password is #AUR3-20

Points to remember when you get a call from Ofsted:

- Try and find a quiet place to receive the call.
- Remain calm.
- Be polite and professional.
- Stay positive and your confidence will shine through.
- Ask for their name and record the details.
- Ask for their car details as this will help with any car parking issues, in case, there is a space constraint in your setting.
- Ask them if they require lunch. Usually, an inspector will take some time off to eat their lunch, particularly when the inspection is a day-long process. This gives them and you some time for a breather. They are human after all!
- Ensure your documentation is ready for the day of inspection.

Documentation checklist

We have prepared a documentation checklist which you will need to have ready on the day of inspection.

Being prepared for this will make it easier for you to stand out whilst also enabling the inspector to spend more time with the children and staff to make observations.

This will help you to excel, look confident and organised.

If easier we have written this here for you:

- Current staff list and qualifications (including first aid and safeguarding certificates.
- A list of children with their date of birth on roll.
- Your staff rota.
- A list of children who will be present on the day of your inspection.
- Disclosure and Barring Service records, your central database with vetting numbers.
- Staff recruitment, application forms, references and the right to work in the UK forms.
- All logs regarding accident, incidents at home and at the setting, medication, behaviour concerns.
- All logs of discrimination, including racism.
- Your complaint log and all the actions from that log.
- Safeguarding and child protection policies.
- Safeguarding log and referrals.
- Fire safety and fire drill log.
- A list of all vulnerable children including English with additional language and children who have additional needs.

Informing the setting

Make sure the whole setting is aware that you are expecting an Early Years inspection, including staff members who might be absent on the day of the call, or the intimation meeting, but are supposed to be working on the day of the inspection. Remember the motto: 'Speed of the leader Speed of the team', all team members need to feel valued and made to feel that they are as much a part of this journey as you are.

Gone are the days when the inspectors would simply arrive on your doorstep unless it's a compliance visit. There is much debate over whether such unannounced check visits are right or wrong. I have been on the receiving end of both and can safely say that the stress of knowing inspectors are coming is far greater than the stress of opening the door to them.

The whole purpose of the call is to clarify the registration status of your setting and any changes made to the registration. These are duly noted and you will need to produce evidence that you have notified Ofsted about the changes on the inspection day.

As an inspector, the most common faux pas I have experienced is with committee-run preschools. The number of times I have arrived at a setting, having pre-checked the portal for the names of nominated persons and committee members, only to find changes on the day. However, Ofsted never received any notification. Note, any change to the committee and to the setting is a reporting requirement and must be reported.

The chair of a committee needs to realise the importance of informing Ofsted of ALL changes. This includes the EY2 form. Failure to do so will impact the grade of your inspection, even before the inspector goes any further to see what a great job you do.

An example of such a report would read like this:

'The provider failed to ensure that the relevant information about new committee members was sent to Ofsted to enable them to complete suitability checks.'

The provider in this case, as it is a committee-run preschool, is the Committee. I cannot stress how important it is for the Committee to understand that they need to have a secure knowledge of their setting.

This could lead to a Grade 3 (*Requires improvement*) or Grade 4 (*Inadequate*) rating, as this discrepancy will impact the safeguarding requirements.

I have stressed this so many times and have noticed now with my training that committee members are now attending this also especially if it is our safeguarding training. This is a huge up levelling in my eyes and feel that committees are now beginning to take on some responsibility for the important job they do.

Check prior to inspection by the inspector

Before the inspection, the inspector will check the following:

- They will check the registration of your setting and confirm the same with you. In case of any ambiguity, the inspector will cross-check with their regional duty desk and try to resolve the issue promptly.
- They will confirm all pieces of information regarding the individuals connected to the registration.
- All information relevant to your setting is stored on their database.
- Any lines of enquiry (LOE) or area of focus (AOF) will be shown on their portal; this includes the recommendations based on previous inspection, any safeguarding concerns and any complaints that may have been recorded. These would also be shown on the portal and the inspector downloads these details

before visiting you. Only Ofsted has access to this information.
- Any previous reports submitted and prepared in connection to your setting.
- Any published information such as any monitoring letters sent out to you. They will check your website in case you have a website.
- If you have a social media page, the inspector will check the page. Please be very mindful of the regulatory due diligence for all the information you upload on your page. For instance, if you are showing the faces of children, the inspector will want to confirm that you have secured written parental permission.

Please do remember that your personal page does have a link to your business page. Whatever is put on your social media page will be shared worldwide. Think about how this may look to the public.

You will also need to speak to the parents and inform them that you are having an inspection.

Parents need to be given the chance to speak to the Ofsted inspector. As one of the reporting requirements, this is indicative of a good working partnership. Your inspector needs to be able to write how well you work with parents and others. If your parents are unable to talk to the Ofsted inspector, why not ask them to write you a testimonial?

As I am writing this obviously parents are not entering into the setting. Actually, some may be but I know inspectors are calling parents on the day if they are unable to meet face-to-face to ask parents how you have worked in partnership with them especially since the pandemic.

It all builds to the body evidence and forms part of you evaluating your practice (see Chapter 2).

Tips for the day of inspection:

- Do not panic.
- Be prepared.
- Breathe.
- Remember through the eyes of a child.
- Remember that you know your children well, you just need to explain the same to the Ofsted inspector. They do not know the children at all, so will want to know what you know.
- Think about if the Ofsted inspector was asked to be the key person to your children instead of you on a particular day; would they know which stage the child is at based on your quality of teaching and children's learning.
- How well your staff team know their curriculum and is it sequenced.

This is a really important aspect to be aware of... all children need to be observed, assessed, and planned for at all times. There should be no gaps in their learning.

On the day

When the inspector arrives, they will introduce themselves and show their identification. In case they do not, please ensure you ask to see their credentials. Also, if you wish to contact Ofsted to confirm this, you have every right.

The inspector will then inform you of the plan of the day. They will also want to:

- Check the accuracy of the information they have on your setting.
- Gather any information regarding staff absences, and details such as how many children you have on roll.
- If you have not placed the notification of inspection on your entrance, then please ensure that you do, so parents and visitors are able to view this.
- Agree on the timetable for inspection activities, a walk around the setting, joint observations and any trips or visits that would be happening during the day.
- Allot time to speak to parents - this may be first due to the timings of parents visiting the setting.
- Allot time for Leadership and Management interview. However I do say that that if you have a really substantial Learning Walk this will be shortened as you will have given so much information during that time.
- Check staff qualifications and record them as evidence.
- Arrangements for feedback - any other individuals you wish to be present.

If you have an unannounced inspection, your inspector will refer to any concerns (which may have been recorded in the previous visits) that have led them to inspect your setting without being notified.

On some occasions, you will be inspected by two inspectors. There are a few reasons for this:

1. The main inspector may be having their Quality Assurance visit by a senior inspector.
2. The main inspector is being shadowed by a new inspector in training.
3. The main inspector will need to have a few inspections under their belt before they are signed off as competent.

Treat these inspectors as you would any inspector.

Shine throughout the day.

With the Education Inspection Framework September 2019 there has been much conversation regarding the amount of data that should be gathered and collated in each setting. Please be mindful of this and demonstrate you know where your children are in their ages and stages of development. See the chapter next on Quality of Education for more details and guidance.

5

THE LEARNING WALK

So, this part of the process which is key to your inspection. So much so I have made this its own chapter as it is so important

I can honestly say that this is one of the most important parts to get right. It is telling your settings story and why you do what you do.

Key pointers to a successful learning walk include the following:

- Practice your learning walk on a regular basis. The reason being is that when it comes to the day it will seem natural to you and your team and so what flows off your tongue is what you are good at and know. There is nothing worse than getting tongue-tied when you speak to an inspector. Believe you me, I've been there many times.

- Encourage the team to do a learning walk too. The reason is that they can then see what you see when they do it. So, when it comes to you doing it again, they would be spot on, and it would flow even better.
- Introduce your team leaders/room managers to the inspector. Hand over some of the responsibility to them. The inspection is a team effort and this needs to be used as a training tool. You are giving them autonomy to talk about their room and their children. It isn't your room it is theirs and they know it best.
- Encourage your room managers to talk about what the intention of the day is. What is it they want to get from today to ensure they are adding impact? What is it they intend the children to learn? So, what you want them to say is and this maybe a little scripted, but it works so go with me on this one.

Child A

The child in question- Sinah and he is 32 months and based in the preschool room.

He loves being outside and adores his dinosaurs that he brings in a different one every day.

You want your staff to say:

'From the last observation I have noticed that Sinah is able to count to 5. I know what him to learn how to count to 10 and practice this. He loves dinosaurs, in fact he brings a different one in every day, and we learn about what the dinosaur is, and he adores being outside so I have created an activity which he will love where I have placed numbers of spots on the dinosaurs, and he is able to match with the recognising the numbers. He is also at the age when he is struggling with sharing, so I am going to work alongside him to help him see that taking turns in the game is a good idea.'

Or another example:

Child B

The child in question is 7 months old and her name is Mollie

Mollie is based in the baby room and has been attending for 8 weeks... she does three days per week.

'From the last observation I noticed that Mollie can now roll over onto her tummy. She uses her legs to kick over and rollover. I am now going to encourage her to reach out and try and grab some of her favourite toys so she can start using the muscles in her arms and body more.'

This is perfect for understanding your curriculum. What you have said it that you have recognised where your key child is, and you now know what you need to do for their next steps and what you want them to learn through their interests.

Practice this exercise daily choosing a different child each day. It certainly helps when we have been visiting settings.

Another tip for your learning walk is talking about how you find out about what child knows and can do when they first join. So, this is also true when a child is transitioning from one room to another. How do you gather this information? Where do you get it from? Is it from their parents or carers? How true is this picture of when they arrive with you? How soon do you do a baseline?

I would always recommend that you encourage parents to tell you where they think their child is. There are several ways in which you can do this. Either have that conversation on settling in visits or encourage them to write it down so you have the evidence. I would not just rely on parents/carers for this information as you know as well as I do that as parents our children are amazing and can-do way more than what they can do for other people!

The other useful tool is from the Foundation Years. I will place this on the website for you to have a look at, but it has been updated from September 2021 in line with the new EYFS – it is called 'What to expect in the EYFS"

Here is the link for you again:

www.jigsawearlyyearsconsultancy.com/are-you-ready-for-your-inspection-book-downloads/

the password is #AUR3-2022

1. Think about how you consider children's experiences and activities that you offer in how you decide what

they learn next. How do you find out about their past experiences, where they come from, etc? This is a great link to Cultural Capital which does not get you stressed when you are asked. We talk further about Cultural Capital in the Quality of Education chapter. Your inspector will not want to see a display board with this on as this has no impact at all.

2. When you are delivering your learning walk this is about what you offer in your setting that has a huge impact on children and that they are making progress (this is the impact). Take the time now after you have read this and walk through your setting, or even better get the staff team on board and at your staff meeting ask them what they feel children get from being in their room. Let them take ownership so it doesn't just fall onto your shoulders.

3. You will need to make the inspector aware and ideally on your learning walk about how you support all children with EAL and SEND. How you have recognised that some children have extra needs and what have you done to ensure those next steps are being achieved. Now is not the time to say, 'Well we haven't heard back from the LA, and we don't know what to do.' This is just going to give yourself a recommendation. When we mean EAL we mean bilingual children also. When you get the notification call you will get asked how many children do you have in each category on the day and overall so this will give you a clue that inspectors are going to be observing and talking to vulnerable children who need more support to ensure that when they leave you they are on an even keel, or they have got the support they need while they are in your care.

4. You will need to talk about what you have done over the past two years during the pandemic to support children's development and their individual needs. How have you coped with working with outside agencies and parents when they have not been able to enter your setting?
5. As you are walking around showcasing your setting and shining... which is what I am hoping you are doing, think about this question and add this along the way. What are you doing to support your staff workload? What is it that you are doing to ensure their well-being is being supported? And what I mean by this is not just the glorified good basket in the staff room which we all love but what are you doing to support them emotional, not physically? Do you catch up, how do you support them and how often, is this recorded? With the pandemic mental well-being is at an all-time low. And I mean low, and this is not only for our staff team but for us also. So, what do you all do as a team to support each other?
6. The focus on children's communication and language is of high priority. It always has been, however, since the pandemic it has hit an all-time low in children's development and where they are. This is not surprising after the time children have been at home while parents are still working alongside conversations have not been had and there has been an increase in children accessing iPads and the television to keep them entertained. It is our crucial role in Early Years to recognise this and put plans in place to help support children in this area of their development. So, during your learning walk, talk

about what you are doing to help support children become confident speakers.
7. Working in partnerships with parents/carers and outside agencies is also key especially since we have been unable to have those face-to-face conversations with those who not only work with children but are closest to them. So, as you are walking around the setting visiting room to room talk about the partnerships you have in place and how with other providers, agencies, schools, this has had a positive impact on children's learning. Focus on the positive side and not the side when you can't get access to them.
8. Think about how you have involved the community in your setting. Think about what you did pre-Covid and what you have done during and after. Think about how the pandemic has affected children particularly disadvantaged in your setting and what you are doing, have done to ensure that their needs are being met fully. How did you encourage them to carry on coming to the setting when it was closed to others? How did you use this time wisely to help those children and families in need? Can you prove what you did? Showcase this, remember if you don't tell the inspector no-one else will! Think about what you did to support parents with their children's learning at home. Did you send activity bags home, emails with ideas of what to do, record stories for children? What did you do to work in partnership with parents to ensure children carried on with their learning when they were absent from your setting?
9. Finally, the most important one, is self-evaluation and we discuss this in another chapter. What have you

identified needs improving and what plans are in place to ensure this is happening and being actioned? Are all staff on board, how do you ensure they are? What about the views of parents and children? How do you do this and ensure that parents are feeling they are being listened to.

6

QUALITY OF EDUCATION

Previously known as Teaching, Learning, and Assessment, the Education Inspection Framework (2019) has changed to Quality of Education. The reason behind this was because Ofsted felt this was overly reliant on outcomes and the supporting data which we had to produce.

Please be mindful, this does not mean that data is taken away. Think about how you can evidence the starting points for a child, or his current stage.

Throughout this chapter, we will focus on what your inspector will want to see and what they will do to make sure you are having an impact on children's learning through your teaching.

I have still retained several subheadings from the previous Teaching, Learning, and Assessment; however, I have also used segregation into relevant sections using new aspects within Quality of Education.

I have now added another section into this chapter.

Curriculum

In simple terms... for people like me... curriculum is what you are wanting a child to learn.

What is the intention for that day?

As of September 2021, the new Early Years Foundation Stage (EYFS) came into place and with this new framework comes confusion, anxiety, and stress for nurseries, preschools and childminders around the UK.

So let us get some facts right first.

You have a choice now. This is probably this biggest reason for the anxiety is that we have a choice and we don't know what to choose or how to choose based on what is easiest for us.

You can follow Development Matters or Birth to Five or you can create your own. Now this is where Early Years settings are getting anxious and scared as there is no guidance out there to show you how you can do you own. So, my advice is read on and make your own informed decision. It must work for your staff team as well as for your children.

So here we go.

Development Matters

This is a non-statutory curriculum guidance for the Early Years Foundation Stage and was commissioned by the Department for Education to work alongside the statutory framework which was released in September 2021. Development Matters is for all Early Years practitioners. It is helping you view how a child learns and develops. It can help you design your own curriculum, but it can also give you the chance to use theirs. It does not replace, as like with any curriculum, our own professional judgement. And this is so important.

It meets the needs and requirements of the framework for the Early Years Foundation stage (EYFS) which we all know we must abide by. It talks about children's experiences, what they do and what they need to learn to do.

Development Matters is a guidance that sets out children's development in ages in stages and this is what we are used to. We do know that not every child follows that pathway and that's where our professional judgement comes into play. It is not supposed to be a tick list, however, if you are like me and like to tick off and see what I need to do next then there is no stopping you from doing this.

We can use our own professional judgment to help children make the right next steps of their learning.

What Development Matters states is the following:

"The curriculum: what we want children to learn.

The curriculum is a top-level plan of everything the Early Years setting wants the children to learn.

Planning to help every child to develop their language is vital.

The curriculum needs to be ambitious. Careful sequencing will help children to build their learning over time.

Young children's learning is often driven by their interests. Plans need to be flexible.

Babies and young children do not develop in a fixed way. Their development is like a spider's web with many strands, not a straight line.

Depth in early learning is much more important than covering lots of things in a superficial way."

Development Matters has seven features of effective practice to help you in your setting to work towards. The three prime areas of learning that underpin everything in the early years:

Communication & Language

Personal, Social and Emotional Development and Physical Development

The four specific areas help children to strengthen then apply the prime areas:

- Literacy
- Mathematics
- Understanding the World
- Expressive Arts and Design

(There is not difference to what the previous Development Matters stated).

These seven areas are not sub-divided into different aspects/strands within Development Matters, although the ELGs with the Statutory Framework 2021 are.

There are three developmental stages:

- Birth to three – babies, toddlers and young children
- Three and four year olds
- Reception

Birth to Five

The other non-statutory guidance which is out there for you to peruse after is Birth to Five Matters. Now this was created as a guidance by 16 organisations in the sector for the sector.

It has six foundations to work with to provide a high-quality provision for children.

It is based around The Unique Child – what a child might be doing, Positive relationships – what adults might do, Enabling environments – what adults might provide, and Learning and Development.

Prime areas of development and learning lay vital foundations in the early years:

Personal, Social and Emotional Development

- Making Relationships
- Sense of Self
- Understanding Feelings

Communication & Language

- Listening and Attention
- Understanding
- Speaking

Physical Development

- Moving and Handling
- Health and Self-Care

Literacy

- Reading

Mathematics

Understanding the World

- People and Communities
- The World
- Technology

Expressive Arts and Design

- Creating with Materials
- Being Imaginative and Expressive

(These aspects/strands do not all correspond with those in the Statutory Framework 2021).

There are six age ranges: from Range 1 to Range 6.

So now I have summarised both those non statutory guidance you can see why settings have become anxious.

The next option is you create your own.

At Jigsaw we would already need over three pairs of hands to count the numerous calls we have received asking our advice and pleading with us to develop training on the EYFS. But with regards to the training our answer is always, "We're afraid not". This is not because we lack the knowledge, it is because we do not want you to pay for something which you already know.

There are minimal changes in the new framework and nothing that providers should be getting stressed out about, by the time you have finished reading this we hope you will breathe a sigh of relief and embrace the changes in a positive way.

Development Matters and Birth to Five can be used as guidance tools to ensure that children are learning and developing. You have the choice of using either, but also the freedom of designing your own should you wish. This news is blooming awesome in our opinion!

But how? This is the recurring question providers are asking in our monthly webinars and mastermind sessions.

Our advice is to break it down into steps, you can create your own bespoke curriculum which ensures your children are learning every day and achieving what they need to with your staff team being the facilitators.

Take a room at a time, ask them to define the age of the children in their room and think about what they feel children of this age need to learn. I.e. if this is babies, then learning to crawl, learning to pull themselves up. Write a list of 10-20 statements that your team feel children need to learn. Then think about resources they would need to help with this.

So, your own curriculum is what you want a child to learn. Next comes the intention, this is where you start thinking about the 3 I's, the intent, the implementation, and the impact. The 3 I's are paramount to the way a child learns, the way a practitioner facilitates and the result. The impact!

Ensure that the whole team are on board and know the importance and key areas of child development. We have seen so many students over the years in our varying roles as managers, lecturers, and inspectors, who have not understood the importance of child development and what this means. Key points to achieve understanding are listed below.

1: Ensure all your team in each room are on board. Look at the level of experience in each room and use everyone to contribute. It is the only way to make a change to ensure that all are on the same wavelength and working towards the common goal of adding impact.

2: In the group, ask them to write what they think a child of that age group needs to learn. Remember and reinforce the prime areas are for only under twos and the prime and specific areas for the over twos - look at the prime area first and foremost.

3: Devise a list of statements that you feel children need to learn before they move on to the next age bracket. Ticking of statements is sometimes the way forward. We know many of you will read this and say, 'Ofsted say they want to reduce the paperwork', and yes, they do, and this can only happen if ALL your key people know their key children well. If you can guarantee they do, then statements are not needed BUT... There is nothing wrong with having something written down, so you are fully aware of each child's needs.

. . .

4: Link each of the statements with the area of learning. For example, Babies: While lying on tummy they are able to push up on arms (PD): Shows interest in faces (CL, PSED).

And that is it, remember that children learn using the Characteristics of Effective learning and your staff team need to be reminded of this.

For example:

- Our children will be able to learn these by us following their CoEL
- Playing and Exploring - engagement - HAND
- Active Learning - motivation - HEART
- Creating and thinking critically -Thinking HEAD

It is as simple as that. Your children are unique, you recognise what they need to learn, and you create their curriculum, their intent.

3 I's and Cultural Capital

The Quality of Education is now broken into three different aspects which the inspector will want to see.

These are:

INTENT

IMPLEMENTATION

IMPACT

So, with this in mind, we will break this down further so you are fully aware of what you need to know.

Firstly, let me just reinforce this to you. Each of those aspects, the 3 I's, are not being graded separately. Instead, inspectors will reach a single grade judgement for the Quality of Education, by gathering all the evidence they have seen, using their professional judgement.

In addition, using their professional judgement, the inspector will also consider the ages, development, and stages of children in the setting.

Whatever you do please do not get hung up on this formula - It is an amazing formula that works, and it will help you see the whole purpose of why you are doing what you are doing. In fact, so much so I personally believe if you took this to the other areas you will have the most perfect evaluation tool. (See the last chapter.)

INTENT

This is all about what you want children to learn. What is the purpose of your teaching? What is the curriculum (EYFS), which you want the children to learn and develop? So, you can see here where the curriculum fits into its place.

Every day, you have a plan for each child on what you want him/her to learn. Every day you have a plan of what you want to teach the child. So, use the child's plan to enhance your plan and meet the collaborative end result - the impact.

Whether it is to encourage a child to be independent in their self-help skills, using scissors, pouring their own drinks, understanding more mathematical concepts, increasing their vocabulary - there is an intention every day.

IMPLEMENTATION

This is all about how you implement your curriculum, that is, the EYFS?

How are you ensuring that children are making progress in all of the seven areas of learning?

This will draw from the intention you had earlier. So, in context of the intent, consider how you are going to implement this, what and how are you going to get the children to achieve this? Are you going to create an adult-led activity to see if a child can use scissors, develop pouring skills using the sand and water tray, create a mathematical shape hunt, read a story, and engage with further sounds to increase children's vocabulary? Ensure you are using children's interest when you are planning for them. This is important.

IMPACT

So, you have implemented your intention – now what?

This is the best aspect!

What IMPACT has this activity, this intention had on children's learning and development? Was there a result?

What was the result?

Needless to say, there does not need to be a result which is positive! Yes, this is where your intention comes full circle, and you think about what and how you want a child to reach that intention.

How do you evaluate the impact of the curriculum you are teaching? How do you find out what children can and cannot do?

How do you assess their knowledge and development levels and stages?

This is a cycle of events, which will help you and children evaluate their achievement. Think about, SO WHAT!

What is the purpose of your activity and how can an IMPACT be achieved and what is its result on children.

Try and remember this when you are planning.

The implementation of your intention will give you the impact.

Inspectors will observe and have conversations with the leaders to find out the intentions of the settings and if they are being met. They will want to know if these intentions are adequately comprehensive and challenging enough for children.

Inspectors will want to see how you use any additional funding, which does include the Early Years Pupil Premium and measure the impact on disadvantaged children's outcomes.

At various platforms including draft consultation, Ofsted seminars and conferences, it has been expressed that data will be minimal in the new framework. I cannot stress enough, this does not mean to stop tracking your children, it does not mean to stop assessing, only because this term has been removed from the title of this area.

Think about this - How else are you going to know where a child is in their learning if you do not know where they started from, how else are you going to know what is their next stage in learning? Please do not stop tracking! It is the only way to demonstrate your awareness of the child's development with an accurate idea of the learning level and development stage.

Effectiveness assessment

Throughout the day, the inspector will judge the effectiveness of your Quality of Education by evaluating the extent to which:

1. You can show what a child is able to achieve in your setting. This must also include children who are not exceeding in their development. If they are exceeding, your inspector will want to see that you are continually demonstrating that the child is making progress and that you are working proactively to ensure that they do not fall behind in their development.
2. You can show to the inspector that you understand the age group you are working with. Conversations will be oriented towards finding out how well you know your key child and what is the next stage of their development - your INTENT, how you are going to IMPLEMENT your intent.
3. Baseline assessments are taken from when a child starts, which includes parents' views and other providers such as preschools, childminders, and day nurseries that the child may have attended.
4. The assessments you are writing for the child are used to plan for the next stage of learning; this can identify children who need extra support in order to help them do well.
5. You can show how you interact and encourage

children to facilitate their development using questioning and critical thinking.
6. You can show how parents understand the progress of their children and how they can contribute and support their child's learning.
7. You can show you recognise diversity and encourage equality of opportunity throughout your learning and teaching at the setting.
8. You are able to prove that the teaching you are incorporating helps children secure skills and develop/learn successfully. This will ensure they are able to be ready for school.

Throughout the day, the Early Years inspector will want to see how effective your teaching is to ensure the growth and development of children using the characteristics of effective learning.

The key evidence that you will need to show is how well children are:

- Playing and exploring.
- Being active in their learning.
- Being able to think critically and be creative.

You will need to show how you evaluate your teaching to support children's learning and ensure that you are aware of the stages and ages of your children in your setting.

'Children's learning is meticulously planned and is informed by the regular and precise assessments of their development. Staff constantly reshapes activities to help children to develop their concentration skills and to motivate them to keep trying. Staffs

are skilled and confident in knowing when to allow time for children to lead their own learning.'

Little Learners, Corby

Your inspector will want to observe how children interact with each other, including with you and your staff, as well as how this will impact their progress.

Progressive check

This does include the Progress Check at 2, parent contributions, and also the summative reports which are shared when children leave for school. From your assessment in your setting, the inspector will want to see that you are able to plan effectively and encourage the traits of effective learning. They will also want to see the impact of your staff's qualification, knowledge, training along with their own learning and development. The quality of all activities in each age group will be considered based on their efficacy.

- So, when a child starts with you, what do you do to gather all the right information?
- Do parents and key people complete a *All about me* form which asks for details to explain the child's interests?
- Do you encourage parents to highlight where they think a child is in their stage of learning?
- If so, how do you do this and what IMPACT does it have on children's outcomes?

Think back to what I mentioned within the Learning Walk chapter. Think about what you have done since March 2020 and how you have ensured you have all the details, interests, learning and development of children when they arrived at your setting. Even if they have left for a long period of time during lockdown, what have you done to ensure the impact of learning is of high priority?

Your inspector will want to see any evidence gathered from children's starting points, often called baseline, and this can also be gained by talking to both practitioners and parents about the level of children's social, communication, and physical skills upon entering the setting and how these are observed when they are still new into the setting.

The inspector will use this evidence to evaluate how well you know about and understand the progress children are making towards the early learning goals. The inspector must judge whether the adults' expectations for children are adequately defined whilst also seeing how confident you are in children's development.

In addition, the inspector will want to see children who are disadvantaged and those who are under-achieving or are catching up quickly. How do you monitor and ensure this is happening?

How to ensure that this is being assessed and written correctly? How often do you evaluate the checks?

Now I know you will be reading this and saying Ofsted are saying less paperwork and will not be checking assessments. I am hearing you BUT can you guarantee that all of your staff team know where a child is and is able to talk about them? If not, then assessments and tracking is important and I personally recommend you do not give this up.

I want to give you a scenario of when I visited a setting and the toddler room they needed seven staff members. They did have seven staff members however, five of them were agency staff. Now this is no disrespect to agency staff but these staff did not know where a child was or needed to be. They had no idea of the curriculum or the intention for any children. When I approached the person who was looking after a certain key child their response was, 'I am agency I do not know.'

I am sorry, but whether you are a permanent member of the team or agency you are still required to know where a child is and what you are wanting them to learn. This is fact. I know that while I am writing this I am seeing and hearing that recruitment is at an all-time low in the Early Years sector and agency staff are being used. But please ensure those agency staff have the best intentions for those children on the day. Otherwise this is almost guaranteed to end up with a grade you do not want.

The Early Years Foundation Stage (EYFS, 2017) requires that parents and carers must be supplied with a short-written summary of their child's development in the three prime learning and development areas of the EYFS:

- Personal, Social and Emotional Development
- Physical Development
- Communication and Language

This happens ideally around two years four months and its purpose is to support practitioners, parents, as well as other outside agencies to see where a child is and enable early identification of any developmental needs so that additional support may be sought.

You need to remember that there is no particular format which needs to be recorded, but only the information which needs to be provided for the prime areas. Beyond the prime areas, it is for practitioners to decide what the written summary should include, reflecting the development level and needs of the individual child and if they need additional support.

The Statutory framework (2021) states:

'It **must** describe the activities and strategies the provider intends to adopt to address any issues or concerns. If a child moves settings between the ages of two and three it is expected that the progress check would usually be undertaken by the setting

where the child has spent most time. Practitioners must discuss with parents and/or carers how the summary of development can be used to support learning at home.'

We asked to see these when we do our Quality Improvement Audits, be aware that these still need to be done whether we were in lockdown or not.

Aims of The Progress Check

- Enable you as a practitioner to understand a child's needs and effectively plan for them.
- Review a child exclusively in the three prime areas.
- Provide parents with a clear understanding of their child's stage of development.
- Enable parents to support children at home to enhance their learning.
- Support your intentions with optimal actions to ensure the children achieve their milestones.

The Progress Check at 2 should be completed by the key person who should know the child really well. They must use their observations in the setting to assess the stage of the child's knowledge, how they understand what they are learning and their behaviour - whilst also considering the views of parents as well as other practitioners such as the inclusion office, if necessary, in the setting.

You will need to explain to the inspector what you do with this information and the details of the information network.

So, think about this information.

Who do you give the report to? Is it just to the parents or carers of the child? If it is why do you only give this to either one of them and not both?

Every child has a Health Visitor who also completes a check at 2 which is recorded. What impact would it have if you sent a copy of the progress at 2 not only to parents but also to the Health Visitor? This is an excellent way of demonstrating how well you work in partnership with others and would serve as a great example of explaining to your inspector that you are proactive enough to work with others at all times in order to meet the needs of children.

If you have any children with additional needs, you need to be able to demonstrate how you are supporting the progress of these children. This is again a very important point. All outcomes need to be consistent in all areas and if not, you will need to explain why not and what/how you are intending to improve upon these.

Children who speak English as an additional language need to be able to gain the skills they need to communicate effectively. Again, think about how you do this in your setting, what is your intention and the impact of how you implement the intention?

Your inspector will evaluate the children's outcomes and take account of children who have made typical progress (or more) from their starting points. An example of typical progress for a child would be that they consistently display the knowledge, skills, and understanding appropriate to their age. They would also be moving steadily towards the early learning goals, which is evidenced through your assessment records of those children.

Children who commence at a lower level of development than is typical for their age should be seen to be able to catch up and make steady progress. A child joining the setting at a higher level of development than would be typical must be given challenges to deepen their learning; this personalised individual achievement is very important.

Every child needs to be focused on by their key person - and assessments, observations and activities need to be able to show that you are meeting every child's unique needs.

Through the day, the inspector will want to observe children's learning and the way staff members interact with children throughout each of those activities.

I have decided after much focus on the new framework to still retain details about Teaching, Learning, and Assessment as it comes under the umbrella of Quality of Education to give you a better understanding of what is to be expected during the inspection process.

Things to remember during your inspection day:

The Early Years inspection handbook for Ofsted registered provision (2019: pg 33) states in the outstanding descriptors:

'The provider meets all the criteria for a good quality of education securely and consistently.

The quality of education at this setting is exceptional.

In addition, the following apply.

- The provider's curriculum **intent** and **implementation** are embedded securely and consistently across the provision. It is evident from what practitioners do that they have a firm and common understanding of the provider's curriculum intent and what it means for their practice. Across all parts of the provision, practitioners' interactions with children are of a high quality and contribute well to delivering the curriculum intent.
- Children's experiences over time are consistently and coherently arranged to build cumulatively sufficient knowledge and skills for their future learning.
- The **impact** of the curriculum on what children know, can remember and do is highly effective. Children demonstrate this through being deeply engaged in their work and play and sustain high levels of concentration. Children, including those children from disadvantaged backgrounds, do well. Children with SEND achieve the best possible outcomes.
- Children consistently use new vocabulary that enables them to communicate effectively. They speak with increasing confidence and fluency, which means that they secure strong foundations for future learning, especially in preparation for them to become fluent readers.'

Clearly, consistency in everything you do in your setting. You cannot achieve *outstanding* unless you are consistent with your exceptional practice across all of your rooms, all of your staff as well as in engaging all of your parents.

Think about this... You are only as strong as your weakest link. Every setting has a weak link and I highly recommend that after reading this you focus on that person. Firstly, let me get this straight. Being weak may not be because they are just not engaging as much as you would like them to. This may mean they need extra training, they may be shy, they may not feel confident in their role. It is your job to help them to grow. FACT. That is indeed the manager's job - to improve on staffs' ability to help children achieve the best outcomes.

Evaluation checklist

As we have said before there are many free resources for you to access through our website. We have taken time to create them for you as we know time is short in Early Years.

Visit using this link:

www.jigsawearlyyearsconsultancy.com/are-you-ready-for-your-inspection-book-downloads/

The password is #AUR3-2022

Activity for you to do to check your staff team are all on board. Invest an entire day (today) to look at the activities that you are providing and setting up for your children. Taking this time will help you reflect on what you have and what you need to change.

- Do you have an intention of the day? (This is meaning the curriculum.)
- Where have you got this intention from? (Ideally you want from last observation.)
- Do you know if and how you are going to implement your intention? (Using the children's interests.)
- Do you feel you can improve upon the intentions?
- How do you evaluate your activities and your continuous provision or your environment?
- What was the impact of the activity?
- Do you get all staff involved?
- Do you get the children involved and using their voices?
- If not, again what is stopping you?

Children need to be involved with their setting. They are the ones that are learning throughout the day. If you are not questioning, facilitating, investigating, communicating with children to extend their learning, then you should be thinking:

Is this the right job for me?

Your inspector cannot show they have preferred practice when they inspect and cannot offer any advice. This was one of the areas I found hard when I was inspecting. I could give recommendations but advice throughout the day was frowned upon, and this led to the establishment of Jigsaw Early Years Consultancy Ltd.

As long as you are showing that the things you are doing are having a positive impact on children's learning and development, you will be good.

There is much debate about how we should plan. To be able to plan 'in the moment' for children, you need to get the basics right first. The Statutory Framework for the Early Years Foundation Stage (2017) states:

*The **learning and development requirements** cover:*

- *the **areas of learning and development** which must shape activities and experiences (**educational programmes**) for children in all Early Years settings.*
- *the **early learning goals** that providers must help children work towards (the knowledge, skills and understanding children should have at the end of the academic year in which they turn five).*
- ***assessment arrangements** for measuring progress (and requirements for reporting to parents and/or carers).'*

The term teaching can sometimes be contrived as a formal way of working. It covers a wide umbrella of ways in which practitioners can help children learn. During some of my inspections, I have had conversations with childminders who say they are not teachers as I have briefly mentioned before but I am afraid that this statement is not quite true. As parents, we are teachers and as practitioners we are teachers; yet, we are also facilitators.

We facilitate children's learning and play through planned and child-initiated activities. We model our language and communicate with them by demonstrating, explaining, showing, exploring, investigating, encouraging, recalling as well as setting and extending challenges.

We need to take account of the resources we provide, the environment and surroundings as well as the structure of the day. When thinking about the resources, we need to be able to provide a host of different textures, shapes, sizes, and resources that are interpreted in terms of whatever a child wants them to be. It is all about the process and not the end product.

What I do want to say is try not to overcrowd your area. Too much choice leads to too much wandering around by children as they are unable to find something they want to do. Stick with only a few purposeful activities which you know will be engaging. There is nothing worse than you creating an activity which doesn't get used!

The whole point of them being open-ended is that they can become a whole new world for a child. This can be a struggle for the practitioner as they have only known what they know based on their past experience. Think about this.

Take a real apple - write down everything you can to describe the apple and questions to ask about it. When I did this training with my delegates, the number of questions was in the high 40s.

Now take a plastic apple - cross off any questions from your previous list which you cannot ask about the apple you now have. How many questions do you have now?

Now take a printed picture of an apple - cross off any questions which are not suitable for the picture. How many questions do you have?

This type of exercise is so important that encourages you to think about the resources you have in your setting. The more open-ended resources you have, the more thought-provoking questions, critical thinking skills and creativity is being used by children.

Think about our brain for one second. Think of it as a muscle. Just like any other muscle, if we do not use the brain it will waste away.

This is why we need to ensure that we are providing the most effective form of teaching as possible to help children learn and develop. You are the source!

Sustained shared thinking

A good definition of sustained shared thinking is as follows:

'Sustained shared thinking' occurs when two or more individuals 'work together' in an intellectual way to solve a problem, clarify a concept, evaluate an activity, extend a narrative, etc.

Both parties must contribute to the thinking and it must develop and extend the understanding. It was more likely to occur when children were interacting 1:1 with an adult or with a single peer partner and during focussed group work.'

The Effective Provision of Pre-School Education (EPPE) Project (2004)

This gave us a better understanding of the concept called sustained shared thinking. The provision also highlights its significance and how it is fundamental to use this practice as practitioners through our teaching so as to ensure that children are learning.

When a child becomes absorbed in a conversation with a practitioner or their interests are captivated during an activity, this will ignite their learning, use their brain, and provoke further investigation. Children will want to discover more and with the help of you as the facilitator, the learning will begin. The story will begin to unfold and children will begin to ask questions amongst their peers.

Whether it is one-to-one or with a small group, sustained shared thinking can be a powerful tool to provide a connection between all. This, in turn, forms a relationship where children feel nurtured and secure. Opportunities arise to reveal a level of cognitive development, boosting both self-esteem and self-worth. The feeling of being valued is of utmost importance to a child. Hence, personal, social, and emotional well-being is one of the prime areas. We need to get this right and then learning will begin to flow as it should.

The theories about sustained shared thinking contributed to the original EYFS, which explicitly stated that sustained shared thinking should be an integral part of a child's creativity and critical thinking (EYFS 4.3). It is also indirectly described in **all** the areas of learning and development.

When you are planning for children's activities, ask yourself: Do you specifically look at areas they need to be developing and create activities which are aligned with that area of learning?

Why do you do this?

Think about your time and what you want the child to learn.

Throughout my inspections, I have seen activities being facilitated which only cover one specific area of learning. Think about how time-consuming this is and what is it that the child can get from that activity. Or are the zones perfectly labelled to cover all areas of learning? Think about why you do this? If you do this, is it for your benefit or the children's? Do the children develop more with those labelled zones? If not, why do you have them?

It is not an Ofsted requirement for you to have labelled areas. If it is for rich print environments think of other ways you can achieve this? Books for example!

Why not try this at your next staff meeting?

Give an item to each person - only one item and see how they can link it to the different areas of learning. This will not only help with observations but will also make you and your staff think about the activities you are offering and how these can impact your children's development.

Let us take the example of a pen. Brainstorm and write down ALL the areas of learning for which the pen can be used. I use this example in my Quality Improvement Inspections and highly recommend you do this at your staff training. Use the form below to help you with this training exercise.

This will be a good staff meeting exercise to encourage staff to think outside-the-box. The more this is done, the more practitioners will be aware that everything we give a child can encompass all areas of learning.

Things to remember during your inspection day:

EIF (2019) stated in their good grade descriptors:

'Practitioners understand the areas of learning they teach and the way in which young children learn. Leaders provide effective support for staff with less experience and knowledge of teaching.

Think about the following when you are preparing for your inspection:

- Have you planned for all seven areas of learning?
- How are you developing your practitioners to become experts in children's development and learning?
- How do you ensure that the environment is suitable for the age and learning stage of each child?
- How do you ensure that children are engaged consistently?

Inspectors will want to see how you evaluate your teaching in your own setting. What is the IMPACT of what you are doing?

Peer on peer observations

To work on Quality of Education you do need to work on Quality of Teaching.

Do you perform peer on peer observations?

I would highly recommend that you start performing peer on peer observations if you haven't already. This will not only help when you are eventually observed on the inspection day but will also go a long way in ensuring that you are evaluating your staff practice and making recommendations to improve.

In order to make peer observations successful, all practitioners need to be fully involved and be willing to reflect on their own practice. The practitioner does need to have a responsibility to take constructive feedback once the observation is complete. Feedback needs to be given when there are no children around and an ideal way would be to link with staff supervisions.

Key points of peer observations

- Acknowledge your skills, celebrate strengths, and recognise your knowledge.
- Encourage you to identify areas for your continuous professional development.
- Give you accountability to improve your practice.
- Empower you with new ways of working.
- Develop a professional relationship with your peers. (I would highly recommend you perform peer observations on each other if you are a childminder; this is exceptional practice).
- Enable you to upskill your practice.
- Use the information as part of your supervision process.
- Provide reflective evidence for Ofsted and your setting's self-evaluation.

Another examples of this is again on our website for you.

www.jigsawearlyyearsconsultancy.com/are-you-ready-for-your-inspection-book-downloads/

The password is #AUR3-2022

Now we have finished focusing on your teaching practice, let us move on to the way children learn.

During the time your inspector is with you they will want to see how children are read stories, how they sing rhymes and how this helps with their communication and language. What we suggest is you just observe how your staff do this with children. Using these observations create your own story time and rhyme observation sheet.

ARE YOU READY FOR YOUR INSPECTION?

- Does the practitioner maintain eye contact when reading to children?
- Does the practitioner introduce the story?
- Does the practitioner sit at the children's level to make eye contact when reading and singing?
- Does the practitioner encourage participation from the beginning of the story?
- Does the practitioner model language well?
- Does the practitioner repeat words for children to copy?
- Are all children engrossed and engaged in the story or rhyme time?
- Does the practitioner use open-ended questions to create curiosity?
- Does the practitioner ensure all children are involved?
- Are children bored when the practitioner is reading or singing?
- Does the practitioner change her voices and tones to engage children fully?
- Does the practitioner give children time enough to answer questions?
- Does the practitioner encourage all children to be involved?
- Is the practitioner's body language warm and welcoming?
- Are the stories and rhymes age appropriate?

Or visit our website to download yours.

www.jigsawearlyyearsconsultancy.com/are-you-ready-for-your-inspection-book-downloads/

The password is #AUR3-2022

Learning

Now we have talked about this earlier within the curriculum section of the chapter so I won't go over it again but just reinforce to you.

Inspectors will ensure that they are able to evidence the following: Characteristics of Effective Learning through the characteristics of effective teaching. This is paramount to a child's journey within your setting.

They will want to see that children are able to play and explore their surroundings, be active in their learning and are able to think critically while also being creative. Children's outcomes will be met through the art of effective teaching. The impact of your teaching will ensure that you have a secure understanding of children's learning. Through the quality of your activities, you will be able to show that children's development is paramount to everyday practice.

We know that teaching, learning and assessment is collectively referred to as the observation, assessment and planning in the learning cycle. But how effective are these in your setting? These should intersect and work together to demonstrate a tangible IMPACT on children's learning. We cannot effectively do one without the other.

It is a bit like a jigsaw puzzle.

You can have all the pieces placed on your table, but it's what do you do with them that eventually matters.

Do you put the pieces around the outside and then start completing in the middle to make the picture? Or do you randomly take a piece and try and find another that will fit with the one which is in your hand!

Reflective practice

Like a puzzle, you need to have a method to implement your intention - your plan.

Can you honestly say that you do all three aspects of this cycle effectively and are able to maximise impact within your setting? Are you able to show how effectively children are learning through your successful teaching? This self-assessment and review need to be constant throughout your setting, in each age group to build any chances of achieving good or outstanding.

I have been a part of many inspections as an Early Years Inspector and then as a consultant through our Quality Improvement Audits. During this, I have noticed that the three areas do not always work in conjunction with each other. This then fails to reflect your teaching in the children's learning and within the assessments, you are writing. Again, if you are not showing any impact this will affect your overall grade.

If you are not able to show how effectively and consistently you are demonstrating impacting, stop and think why is that?

What do you think is the reason for this?

- Is it a time issue?
- Is it a training issue?
- Is it a monitoring issue?

Or is it all three?

We need to ensure that our practice is reflective and realise that we can improve upon how we deliver to ensure the children's needs are being met constantly.

So let us go back to the basics and talk about the most important - the UNIQUE child.

The understanding of these principles of EYFS is paramount in understanding how a child learns best. We can follow several approaches to help us with the best practice, but it is highly important for us to understand that we cannot implement these approaches without taking into account the needs of our children. Each child in your setting is unique. They all have different learning styles, and their needs are different from each other. Each child has different interests and develops in a unique way. We need to take into account this first before planning our children's learning journey to ensure that we have covered the bare necessities.

Take the time now to reflect upon each child. Use one week to formally not observe, assess or plan for the children in your care; instead, take a step back and follow them everywhere they go.

- Do they have a particular interest in an area of your setting?
- Do they have a schema?
- Do they prefer to be hands-on or just sit back and watch?
- Do they like to get their hands dirty or do they prefer not to partake in the creative activities you have set out?
- Do you need to set out and assign activities, or are children able to choose for themselves?
- Do they encourage their peers to be involved in their play?

This activity is very important to get to know your children and I highly recommend undertaking this activity when you have new children starting with you. Observe their cycle of learning and make notes. This record will help you plan for them eventually and knowing their style can help you out when your inspector asks you to explain about a particular key child. They will want you to tell them everything and demonstrate that you understand their learning journey.

Use the time this week to extensively focus on this. Just one week.

It will not make *any* difference to the assessments of your children; in fact, it will have a positive IMPACT on their learning. Because this exercise will help you gain a better understanding of them as a child.

Carry post-it notes and make intelligent notes of your key child's interests. This will give you a sound basis of knowing what unique means to children within your setting. Use this information to start being the facilitator in the children's story of their time with you.

Once you have the information, observe and record after one week.

Use the first observation after this week as a baseline for where (the stage/level) you think your children are in the learning and development cycle. We will discuss this further in the understanding of assessments.

Positive relationships

Your inspector will want to analyse the relationship you have with children within your setting.

Positive relationships between staff and children are able to give children a feeling of belonging and a sense of self-worth. Relationships need to be warm and loving; the practitioner needs to be ultra-sensitive to a child's needs. They are encouraging, supportive and consistent with their boundaries. These relationships are a clear way of providing ground for heart-felt and stimulating conversations wherein the practitioner becomes a facilitator for the child's needs.

The inspector will want to talk to the children's key person and ask them to talk about a particular child they are observing. They will want the practitioner to know the child's interests, where they currently are in their stages of learning, and what are their next steps. They will also want to observe these steps in day-to-day functioning, to assess if these are impacting a child's learning. This is highly reinforced within the Education Inspection Framework.

The Early Years Foundation Stage (2021) explains that practitioners would do well to be sensitive to a child's needs and respond sensitively to extend their learning and curiosity. By a practitioner observing and tuning in to a child, they will be able to discover what the children like to do, when they are confident in their surroundings and when they are in need of extra guidance.

Effective learning can only be demonstrated when children are being motivated. With motivation, they will begin to show signs of concentrations and will engage in a meaningful play where they are able to use their critical thinking skills, learn from their mistakes and become resilient.

Equally, effective learning can only be determined when practitioners are able to model active listening skills. To that end, the use of eye contact and responses to a child's discoveries begins to have significance.

Think back to when asking a question to a child. How long did you wait for an answer?

Giving children adequate time to answer a question not only ensures that they have a feeling of self-worth, but also encourages their brain to process and respond more effectively to the question. If you keep asking a barrage of questions, the children will tend to only remember the last word you shared with them. It is imperative that practitioners show respect to children and let them learn for themselves in their own unique way.

It is often said that the environment is the third teacher. This idea was postulated by the schools of Reggio Emilia, who opined that the experiences learnt within your environment hold the key to the successful development of the children. Providing resources for children to participate and collaborate with their peers whilst also being facilitated by the practitioner is paramount to holistically embedding learning in a child's day.

Think about your environment and take a glance at areas where children are actively learning. The use of observations will be immensely helpful to evaluate how your children are learning, and which areas are being enthusiastically used and constantly developed by children within their own play and learning. Moreover, open-ended resources are highly effective in a child's day and, as such, need to be actively promoted. Encouraging the children to use awe and wonder to create curiosity in order to develop their own critical thinking and skills provides the basis of vital learning.

Generally, children are born curious and the one thing we all know that in today's society; personal, social and emotional development is high on the agenda of any learning. In order to foster their curiosity, children need to explore the world around them and an open-ended environment gives them just that. It has no pre-determined boundaries and there is no fixed outcome. Children are also able to follow their own imagination and enable their creativity to take them wherever they want to go. Indisputably, this is paramount for learning to take place.

Children learn best through provocations which you provide for them. Over the past few years, the word provocations have been spreading like wildfire.

Do you know what this means?

Firstly, the term originated from the Reggio approach. Put simply, provocation means provoking learning by enticing children to play and encouraging them to be curious, creating awe and wonder to think for themselves. These, in fact, entail all the characteristics of effective learning which we need to aim toward and ensure become known to us within our children's everyday learning.

Now, it is tempting to think that you do this day in and day out by making your setting inviting and enabling children to share their interests; however, these resources need to be open-ended so that children can decide what they want to do, how they want to do it and when they want to do it. Remember children learn more during a process rather than with an end product. However lovely it may be, children need to feel their learning is being valued through their own processes.

Are we being too adult-led? Again, another debatable question. But the fact is children learn best when they are interested in what they want to do, not by what you want them to do!

Curiosity led creativity

In The Art of Thought, Wallas (1926) suggests four processes for curiosity led creativity:

- **Preparation**
- **Simmering/ incubation**
- **Illumination**
- **Verification**

Preparation – when we are being creative, we investigate all areas.

Simmering/incubation – creativity can drift two ways - positive and negative - and it's up to the artist to find helpful solutions by using the brain.

Illumination – after the above two stages, the A-ha or Eureka moment eventually occurs.

Verification – is in creating the creation!

Linking to provocations, we should be making sure that our activities are interesting and original to the child. They need to find for themselves the direction of their choice to make it their original learning. The key here is all about keeping it simple.

Try it. Visit your local scrap store and place the resources around your setting. Do not assign any activity, simply sit back and watch what happens - think about what Wallas has suggested. The art lies in provoking communication and language to get children to think for themselves!

Your inspector will not want to be able to take into account the different approaches or ethos you have in your setting, but they do need to see what a child is learning within your setting.

Think about this.

You can use two tin cans.

Can 1: Is labelled stating what is inside of it. (Tomato soup, in this exercise).

Can 2: There is no label. It is a plain silver tin can.

Which one of the above is going to provoke more curiosity, creativity, critical thinking skills, investigations, discovery, and exploration?

The next time you set activities out for children, use these questions as a tool for your staff:

- What area of learning are children achieving with this activity?
- What skills will the children be using?
- Will this engage and excite children?
- Will this provoke imagination and spark inspiration?
- Will this be a good basis for children to take the activity off to something new?
- What is the IMPACT of the activity?

The involvement in children's learning assumes topmost priority for them to learn. Indicators of such involvement give us vital clues of how children are learning. This self-learning process starts at a very young age - from the time they are babies - where connections to the brain grow and join together to form other connections. Without this, children will not develop.

Emotions, regardless of whether they are positive or negative, have an impact on the way children learn. Negative emotions will not encourage brain neurons to join and will create stress and anxiety in a child's life. This will adversely impact their learning, whereas positive experiences in a child's life will give them the desired hunger to learn more and ensure their life's trajectory is moving forward.

Children have an eagerness to learn and be curious. They delight in being investigators and are able to discover new ways of learning. It is all about the learning process for them, and not merely the desired end-product.

I have been to several inspections where I see end products of what children have created.

Think about this!

Have children produced the Mother's or Father's Day card? What impact did this have on their learning? Why did we do these activities?

Children need to be able to process what they are doing, and this can only be done by allowing and rather facilitating the children to be unique in their own learning. Worksheets are another example of a product of something which the children have not been the original supplier.

Pieces of artwork should be from a child's own perspective and not from ours. It should not be because parents want to see this end result. When you show parents around if you explained to them why each piece of artwork will be individual, this will surely show you are treating each child as their own.

Again, they are UNIQUE.

The point of process over product is that there is no right or wrong way. There are no step-by-step instructions or samples for children to follow. They are able to show their own meanings and there is no right or wrong way to explore or create. The pieces of art produced remain highly focused on the child's experiences and exploration of tools, material, and media.

The whole process will be calm and children will spend much longer creating their own masterpieces. It will be the child's choice. Your inspector will want to see how you are encouraging this type of learning. They will also want to observe the children making choices with confidence within their surroundings. They will want to see practitioners facilitate this style of learning and be able to share their findings with the inspector.

English as an Additional Language

Children who have English as an additional language is currently a hot topic. The inspector will want to see the opportunities you offer to the children to develop and be able to use their home language during their play and learning. In addition, activities should be devised which also support their native language.

The language used in a child's own home needs to be developed in your setting within their learning and development. Much research from Chomsky explains that children learn from their home language early on and are able to extend this learning during their early years.

Within the Education Inspection Framework (2019), it states:

'Practitioners ensure that their own speaking, listening and reading of English enables children to hear and develop their

own language and vocabulary well. They read to children in a way that excites and engages them, introducing new ideas, concepts and vocabulary.'

Your inspector will want to observe practitioners reading stories to children - an exercise, which will create an excitement for language in them and encourage them to remain focused. They will want to observe rhymes and songs to introduce new vocabulary and repetitive words to extend their understanding and learning.

So, look at your staff, are they all good at creating story time and being engaging and inspiring, if not why not? I would highly recommend when you have new staff come for an interview to do a role-play for you or ask them to read a story to some children and observe. Use the observation sheet which is found on our resources section of our website to help you make the decision on whether these are the right practitioners for the children in your setting.

www.jigsawearlyyearsconsultancy.com/are-you-ready-for-your-inspection-book-downloads/

The password is #AUR3-2022

Speaking and communicating with a child is key. If staff do not have that skill then the role is clearly not for them.

During an inspection - early on in my inspection experience, I was able to observe a child enter the preschool and just wander around. I chose this child as I clearly fathomed that he was nervous and zoomed straight to the sand pit.

I observed and recorded his activities for two hours. During that time, he did not move from the sandpit; he did not play with the sand, nor did he build anything. His hands were just placed within the sand and he was gazing around the room.

English was not his first language.

After evidencing my observations, I requested to speak to his key person. They did not know the child's next steps or where they were in their areas of learning. I inevitably got concerned about him. I explained that I had been observing this child for a long period of time and did not find anyone talking to him.

The practitioner looked at me and said she did not know what to say to him as he did not speak English.

Yes, I am still surprised today as I write this, do you also find this alarming?

So not only was the setting aware that English was an additional language for the child, but they also did not know what his next steps were as observations were neither accurate nor recorded effectively to show where he was in his learning.

I asked how they would have felt if no-one spoke to them for two hours. If not one person acknowledged their presence, how would that make them feel? The limited communication and language support for this child surely did not prepare him for school which he was supposed to start within the next few months. Interactions from the staff remained poor and also showed that the opportunities for learning and engaging in worthwhile activities were limited.

Needless to say, this setting did not achieve a positive grading.

Children's home language is very important to provide those critical family links, especially if you have children who are being cared for by older, non-English speaking family members. Between the children and their carers - they need to be able to have purposeful conversations with each other. And as a childminder, it becomes your responsibility to ensure this.

Since writing the first book I have visited many settings and it makes me sad to watch how children who do not have the same language as our own are not focused on to ensure their communication and language skills are being promoted. Not only does this need to be done with conversational skills but it links so clearly to personal, social and emotional development which we will talk about later in the book. So think about this, how would you like it if no one spoke to you for a few hours? How will this make you feel? Remember every child is unique and needs to be treated with that in mind.

Assessment

I have kept this in the book and I will explain the reasons why. Ofsted have said they want us to have less paperwork which is amazing when you say it out loud. However, if you do not have a staff team who are clearly understanding of what is child development then assessment and do I dare say the word tracking (do not shout at me), I would highly recommended.

Throughout the day, the inspector will want to see how you know what a child needs to learn what you have observed? You need to see what has taken place throughout a variety of processes such as examples of children's work through mark making, evidence from any photographs you may have taken, and discussions from parents about things you have not observed before.

Your inspector will want to see where a child was when they started with you.

These are referred to as starting points or baseline assessments.

Practitioners need to ensure that the content, the sequencing and the progression in the areas of learning are secure and that you are demanding enough of children.

This is very important.

Your curriculum needs to be sequenced. The best way to describe this is.

You are at 'A' and you want to get to 'Z'.

You have to travel through B, C, D, E, etc, before you get there... you cannot jump otherwise you are going to miss the opportunities of what B, C, D, E give you.

This may be a simple way of explaining it but it works!

Whenever I have visited settings and asked to see the children's starting points, there has been no consistency in the records. It constitutes a good practice to enable a child to settle in your setting before you set out to track a child. However, you can observe visually from day one and a highly efficient practitioner will begin to build a picture of the child starting from the initial time. They will also start to see a child's likes and dislikes whilst analysing the way they are learning. This, in turn, will ensure that children's unique ways are being taken into consideration during their development.

As part of the starting points' process, we also need to gather information from the parents. How do you do this in your setting? As mentioned previously, parents are the first educator and gaining this information is paramount to working in partnership. The information gathered when a child starts with you can be a good way of gathering much useful information. Using

'All about me' documents as part of the settling in time and gathering at home visits begin to set up a clear picture of a child. See the website resources again for the document you may like to use.

www.jigsawearlyyearsconsultancy.com/are-you-ready-for-your-inspection-book-downloads/

The password is #AUR3-2022

This is such an important time to tell parents how often you will be observing and assessing their children - and how important it is for them to equally contribute. On their part, parents will want to know who is their child's key person; and this early engagement will start to form the much-needed relationship in Early Years settings.

It is also a good practice to ensure that you are meeting the needs of a child and that their starting points are assessed within the first three-week period maximum. This will give you adequate time to consider parental contributions. Using the areas of learning, the key person should be able to make a judgement from their observations to decipher where a child is working within and identify the stages of learning and development through a 'best fit' judgement using your own professional judgement.

Use the headings:

- Beginning
- Developing
- Secure

These will help you prepare the first chapter of a child's journey and ensure that you are meeting their particular needs.

In addition, exceptional practice would be necessary to make sure this is consistent within your setting. Now, for the inspection, think about how can you demonstrate this?

If you are a day nursery, one way that I recommend within my own Quality Improvement Audits is to complete a starting point or baseline assessment at the point of entry to each room. This will not only ensure that children's assessments are kept up to date, but also prove that practitioners are consistent in applying their knowledge of children's development.

Formative assessment and summative assessment

Through the practice of consistent observations over a period of time, the children's own learning story will start to evolve. In companionship with the use of your provocations, invitations and the facilitation of their play, this will result in progress and planning for the next steps. This is called the assessment of learning and is based on the information you need for everyday planning. It is also called formative assessment.

The Statutory framework for Early Years Foundation Stage (2021) states:

'Assessment should not entail prolonged breaks from interaction with children, nor require excessive paperwork. When assessing whether an individual child is at the expected level of development, **practitioners should draw on their knowledge of the child and their own expert professional judgement and should not be required to prove this through collection of physical evidence.*'*

I have highlighted this so you can see that you do not have to have physical evidence, however, this is only if your staff have good professional knowledge of child development.

So with the recruitment crisis as it is in Early Years I would highly recommend that you carry on. If it works don't break it!

Another form of assessment is called summative assessment. This is written by summarising the evidence you have collated from the formative assessments over a period of time. This information is further condensed to share with parents and outside agencies, towards demonstrating children's progress.

If you do these, think about when you write these at this particular time.

The inspector will want to see how you do this and its impact on the children's own learning journey.

Providing this type of assessment is paramount when working in partnership with parents as this serves as a reference guide. This documentation informs them of which stage their child is currently in and how they can help ensure that they are developing, or if any intervention is needed.

It is a good idea to share summative assessments at the end of each term. If practitioners start to give evidence of their understanding of where a child is currently situated, then this will show that they have good knowledge on how to develop and provide the requisite tools for the next stage of learning.

It is important to show you can prove how well versed you are with the uniqueness of each of your key children and their progression to the inspector.

Inspectors will want to find out where starting points are for the child as well as their individual progress. The corresponding evidence must ensure that you are aware of any additional needs and how you are going to ensure these do not have any adverse impact on a child's learning journey.

I want to also clarify the myth that your inspector will not track so I have added what the Early Years Inspection Handbook states (this was updated September 2021):

*'In group provision, the inspector **must** track a representative sample of two or more children across the inspection. The inspector should discuss with the provider what they intend the relevant children to learn and remember based on what those children know and can already do.*

The evidence collected must refer to:

- *the practitioner's knowledge of each child.*
- *the progress check for any children aged two.*
- *the impact of any Early Years pupil premium funding on the children's development.*
- *the quality of support for any children with SEND.*
- *the discussions held with each child's key person and how they decide what to teach.*
- *how well children are developing in the prime and specific areas of learning that help them to be ready for their next stage of education, including school.*
- *the reason why children may not receive their full entitlement to early education and the impact that has on them, particularly those from disadvantaged backgrounds and those with SEND.'*

Inspectors will want to find out about the story of a child, including:

- what they knew and could do when they started at the provision.
- what they can do now and how you got them there.

- what your plans are for that child so that they are ready for their next stage of learning.

Getting to know children and finding out what they know and can do, is something we know Early Years practitioners are skilled at. This is what is important. Whatever you have in place for the assessment of young children shouldn't take adults away from those important interactions. However, practitioners do need to know their key children well. I want to reinforce the use of agency staff also amongst this paragraph. I know recruitment is a huge issue in Early Years and settings are using agency staff. Not only is that having a drain on funds it also has a drain on what children are experiencing. So if you are using agency staff ensure they know what their job is for the day, what their intention is and which the children are they focusing on.

It is highly important to make sure the job of tracking is effective.

Think about the observation cycle and the jigsaw pieces we discussed earlier. You cannot have one without the other.

Whichever way you assess children, whether it is paper-based or using online journals, you will need to show your inspector how confident you are in child development. You will need to know what your key child's next stage in learning is and underpin this plan with adequate reasoning.

By ensuring that children are being taught inspirationally, you can ensure that they are successfully learning. Through the success of their learning, you will be able to assess effectively. It's a cycle, please understand, and you need to show the impact you are making.

Child development tracking

No doubt, Ofsted inspection and guidance are highly important for us. However, they won't judge you on the practice delivery mechanisms in the setting, as it is more essential to demonstrate the impact you are having on your children.

You need to show that you are delivering a welcoming, nurturing and evolving practice that meets the needs and outcomes of all children who walk through your door. You need to grow as a setting and discover what works well for you and your children. You know your children better than anyone else. Remember that. You will have a range of techniques specifically suited to the learning styles of your children and you need to ensure that the quality of each endeavour with the children is of the highest form.

Think back... can you honestly say this is done consistently?

Again, to achieve the *outstanding* grading this needs to be done continually. You need to have achieved the whole of the good criteria in this judgement as well as the *outstanding* criteria. There is now best fit in the new Education Inspection Framework.

By meeting the needs of all the welfare requirements and the Statutory Framework for the Early Years Foundation Stage (2021), you are well on your way to evidencing that you are meeting those needs. Once this has been achieved, you then need to look at your practice little by little to make sure this is effective for all children, and not just the ones who are exceeding.

What about children who need a little help? The invisible child that doesn't give you a stressful day? The one who wanders around the room looking for things to do? Or the one who rarely engages in conversation with you unless you are asking a question… if that is the case, please make sure it's open-ended to extend their learning.

The dreaded joint observation

On the inspection day, the inspector will ask the manager to participate in a joint observation. The purpose of this is to gather evidence on how well the staff members are engaging with children, and how effectively the manager is able to evaluate the observation and make effective recommendations. It does not necessarily have to be the manager of the setting who takes part in the joint observation. In case, you have a teaching and learning member of staff who oversees the overall effectiveness of teaching and learning, they can also observe along with the inspector.

The observation does not necessarily have to be written alongside the inspector. However, it is recommended to make your own notes of your evaluations of the observation, to subsequently share with the team and identify the differences between the inspector and the observer. The inspector will want to see that you are observing what they are observing and a discussion will be undertaken regarding how to improve on the activity and the staff's interaction with the children.

Joint observations are not feasible with childminders who work alone. However, the inspector will want to observe individual children with the childminder and be able to discuss their learning progress/behaviour. At such times, you would want to make use of a volunteer to attend to your role.

This observation is a way of evaluating your practice. Here, one important point I want to draw your attention to is that please do not create an activity just for your inspector to see. This has happened many times during my inspections. Not only does it look false, but the fact is that children never lie, it creates a bad impression of fabricating false scenarios for inspection.

Some pointers when creating activities with children: My senior inspector taught me that everything I know as an inspector.

I need to think 'SO WHAT.' Think what is the INTENT, how am I going to IMPLEMENT this and what is the IMPACT.

So, with that in mind, attempt to adhere to the following guidelines.

Firstly, always engage in activities that would interest your children and this you would be able to identify by working closely with them, as mentioned before. Make a note of their interests as these are ever-changing. Another exceptional way is to engage parents in these activities.

Why not send out this form out to parents every half-term so you are able to work in collaboration with them? This shows an excellent working partnership as children's interests may be different at home to your setting and you will be able to bounce ideas off with each other.

With this collaborative approach, you are also able to choose which activity you wish the inspector to observe with yourself or with your nominated person. If you decide to decline the opportunity; for this to happen, the inspector must record this within their evidence. My recommendation is not to decline this offer. Instead, put this time to good use to showcase your connection with your children.

This is your time to shine and think about whether your decline would be a wasted opportunity to show what your setting does, how well your staff interact with children, the benefits of such activities and the impact it has on the children's development and learning.

So, before the day of the inspection, make sure you have spoken to your staff about what is going to happen on the day and ask your staff if anyone wants to volunteer to be observed. This step not only ensures that all staff members are involved, but it also helps them feel valued and a part of the process.

Think about the types of activity you want the inspector to observe and the interactions staff members have with children.

Quality of education – Self-evaluation

To ensure that you are ready for your inspection, why not start now in measuring how good your quality of education is? What is your intention, how are you going to implement and what is the IMPACT?

Take the time now before your inspection to address concerns you may have. Ensure that all team members are on board as this will show clarity and consistency when your inspection finally happens. Think about the quality of your staff interactions through their teaching.

Do they understand sustained shared thinking and are they able to question the children to perfect those critical thinking skills which are so important in the early stages of a child's life for their optimal development?

Through your own observations monitor the responses of children when being questioned and observe the activities in which they are participating.

- Are they encouraging curiosity?
- Are they thinking about investigating further?
- How is communication and language promoted throughout the activities?
- Are staff members making eye contact with children during these valuable conversations and making children feel valued?
- Are they building from children's knowledge, recalling from previous events and using different teaching methods to suit children's learning styles?

I have been to several inspections and audits where I have observed what it takes to develop an understanding of the observation, assessment and planning cycle. You get this right from today and for the longer term, it is sure to have an infinitely positive impact on children's outcomes and help them prepare better for school.

Do you practice joint observations? If not why not?

Again we have placed a template in the section on our website for you.

www.jigsawearlyyearsconsultancy.com/are-you-ready-for-your-inspection-book-downloads/

The password is #AUR3-2022

At the end of the joint observation, you and the inspector will discuss your collective findings. Just like with any reflections in your setting, it is imperative to understand your practice observations. They help you, the inspector and your team, to gain an understanding of the development of your team. It will demonstrate your knowledge of how children are learning and developing and how you as a manager are aware of how to make progressive improvements.

The observations will be able to assess not only practitioners but also the person who is observing alongside them. They will want to see a good evaluation and how this impacts children as well as the development of staff members.

If you are part of a childminding network, I would use this opportunity to carry out observations on each other, something similar to peer-review. This shows outstanding practice on how to improve on your own development in a practice where you are very much working on your own.

The Education Inspection Handbook (2021) informs us that:

*'The inspector should always invite the provider or a nominated senior member of staff - such as the manager or Early Years professional - to take part in one or more **joint observations** of activities, care routines and/or scrutiny of the progress children make. If the provider declines the opportunity to take part in joint observations, this should be recorded in the evidence base, along with the reason given.*

Joint observations should enable the inspector to:

- *Gain an insight into the effectiveness of the provision's professional development programme for practitioners.*
- *Learn about the provider's view of staff's interactions with children.*
- *See the quality of the implementation of the **curriculum**/educational programmes.*

- *Consider how effectively the manager supports staff to promote the learning and development of all children.'*

If the quality of the practice shows differences and fails to meet the expected standards, it is important that the inspector talks to you about what was observed. The inspector will subsequently want to see how you plan to ensure improvements are being made and how these will be monitored.

You and the inspector will agree on a time to give feedback to the practitioner and manage the situation well. The inspector may seek involvement in this scenario, so they are able to see how you as the manager are performing this task. This is all part of the joint observation and will be recorded within the inspector evidence of the day.

Points to remember:

- Be prepared.
- Ensure you are contributing to peer observations before the inspection, so it becomes a natural process within your day-to-day running.
- Be evaluative. Understand what needs to improve and how you are going to achieve this.

Once you have started using the joint observation format, it will become easier and not come as a total shock when you are expected to do this with your inspector. By ensuring that you and your staff members are comfortable with this process, it becomes natural and this will have an impact on the outcome of your day.

Cultural Capital

There has been much debate surrounding the words Cultural Capital and what it is supposed to mean. Basically, it is *'the essential knowledge that children need - to prepare them for their future success'.*

This is **NOT** another display board that you feel you need to place on the wall because Ofsted want to see. You need to be doing this, every day in your activities, on how well you are enhancing experiences for children and giving them more opportunities - particularly for the most disadvantaged children.

Each child is unique. We know that. Each child enters your setting with a range of experiences that they have already received. However, the range of experiences are unique to each child. As such, it is up to you to create positive experiences in children's learning and play and with the interactions from practitioners, which makes a difference for children. It is your job to create the awe and wonder of the world in which children live, throughout all the seven areas of learning.

So, let me share with you some examples for better clarity.

If you are an Early Years setting which is based in a city, what do you give children to ensure they have the same experiences as children who live in the country?

For example, do children in your setting know about farm animals, the transport in farms, what young babies are from farm animals called, or where eggs and milk come from? It is your job to create those experiences in a setting that ensures that children are ready and prepared to go to school. They should have experienced a wide range of activities to impact and make a difference to their understanding of the world.

Take this time now to reflect on the experiences you provide for your children in your setting and how you enhance their learning for them.

Similarly, if you are an Early Years setting, which is based in the countryside, how do you ensure that children understand about the sea, about mammals and their young, about the plastic pollution of our oceans, about different tides and the textures and smells of seaweed and shells to provoke their senses? Where do fish come from, what do they feel like, how big can they get and what do they eat? This is just another example of how you can look at the experiences you are offering the children to provoke their curiosity and critical thinking.

Please remember this is just one example and you will need to reflect on the children that enter your setting to understand what they have experienced and how you can improve on these to ensure they are ready for their next stage of learning.

It is as simple as that!

Think

INTENT

IMPLEMENTATION

IMPACT

7

BEHAVIOUR AND ATTITUDES

Since March 2020 when we were all in a period of time which seems surreal when you look back, children have either been in the lockdown the same as us or in a setting with minimal children.

When we think about children in lockdown, I want you to think about what they are experiencing when they are at home. Now, I am not saying parent skills are minimal at all but the majority of parents would be still working but at home AND with a child at home too. I don't know about you, but this would make me extremely anxious, and I can assure you that those skills I had as a parent went out the window when I would be trying to work. So, what I am envisaging is that the television and electrical tablets would be out to entertain children so that work could commence. You can see where I am going with this can't you?

So when children are now back in your setting their behaviour has changed. I have seen this in every visit I have been making since April 2020. Children are not knowing how to play with each other, communicate with their peers and know what is right from wrong.

And it is not their fault. In fact, it is nobody's! But the problem is in Early Years we have to solve that problem. Now that is the problem. Are the skills we have in our sector now able to cope with the changes in behaviour in children? I would like to say yes, and I am hoping by the time you are reading this we are seeing a change in recruiting the right staff.

So during the day of inspection, your inspector will make a judgement on children's behaviour and attitudes. This will be demonstrated through the characteristics of effective learning.

The aspects to these we all know is:

- Play and Exploring
- Active Learning
- Creating and thinking critically

Another way of remembering these is:

- Hand
- Heart
- Head

If you would like the free poster of this please visit our website.

www.jigsawearlyyearsconsultancy.com/are-you-ready-for-your-inspection-book-downloads/

The password is #AUR3-2022

Without any of these being integrated within the day's activities, there is no learning. Note, without your effective teaching children will not be learning successfully.

Inspectors will want to see the extent to which practitioners support children's behaviours and attitudes, which does include how children manage their own behaviour.

Inspectors will want to see that children are able to have a sense of achievement of what they are developing in as well as a commitment to learning through the culture of your setting.

Think about how you do that in your setting.

Your inspector will want to see how you promote children's physical and emotional health by monitoring their behaviour and conduct.

Think about how children are able to manage their own feelings as well as convey this to their peers and others. Another useful idea would be to discuss behaviour at a staff meeting in your setting and work out strategies within your team about how you can improve on this if you have any concerns. Document this as this will show you are being evaluative. Make sure you set a target date of when this needs to be achieved.

Did you know that your local authority will be able to help you with any concerns you may have regarding behaviour? I know many of you will be reading this and saying they won't. But please persevere as that is their job to help you. Record every time you try to contact them as evidence that you have been trying. Portage services look at working with families to help them develop and have life experiences for young children. They are able to support parents, settings, and children in minimising barriers that can threaten children and support the services that you can access. Ensuring that you are making accurate observations about children whom you have concerns about regarding their behaviour, is principal to ensuring that all outcomes for children are met. Your inspector will want to see what services you access and how this supports a child's development.

Attendance

Attendance also needs to be monitored in your setting as this not only ensures the safety of children but also builds relationships with their key person. Continuing attendance is extremely paramount to building relationships with staff and children's peers. The inspector will want to see how you monitor and record attendance. They will want to explore how you work with parents to promote children's attendance; this will help children with their future learning when they start school.

Be mindful that you ensure attendance is being recorded effectively. When your inspector arrives, they may well check your register and count the children who are in the room. When was the last time you spot-checked this?

Take some time to just count children in the room and see if they have been marked in on the register. This is highly important to make sure you and your staff register the time and sign in when a child enters and leaves your setting. You have a duty of care to protect children, and this will help ensure you are monitoring this.

I say this as this story happened while I was inspecting a nursery. Something in the kitchen caused the fire alarm to go off. Luckily it was a false alarm because the register was not complete! When the children and staff arrived outside at their fire point, they had more children than marked on their register. My point here is you need to accurately record how many children you have in your setting at any one time. This regulation is essential for protecting children and it must always be adhered to.

Do you get parents to sign their children in with the time and a signature or do you rely on staff to do this?

Whatever way you record this - remember the word impact.

What is the point of you recording this? Remember duty of care as well. Regarding attendance records, do you record the time of arrival and departure of each child? If not, why not?

Safety

Exceptional practice in any setting - whether you are full day care or a childminder - is to be able to demonstrate that the need to ensure safety is paramount and high on the agenda of your setting. Recording the time of children arriving and departing with a signature highlight the duty of care you have to protect children. We all know that you have to maintain records regarding children for a certain number of years, but think about why we do this.

You have a duty to protect children and show how you are going to achieve this.

You will need to be aware of any patterns of absences that may be suggested to other wider safeguarding concerns. Your inspector will look at how well you work in partnership with parents to promote children's good attendance.

Other pieces of evidence also need to be considered during this area of the inspection in terms of how well your policies and procedures are known by practitioners and how these are evident within your setting.

Are you able to demonstrate this being cascaded to staff and are they aware of the implications in case of non-compliance?

Behaviour and attitudes

Again, let us just reinforce that inspectors will need to be able to see that managers and practitioners are able to support children's behaviours and attitudes. This includes how the settings help children to manage their own feelings and behaviour and how they relate to other children.

In order to reach a judgement regarding this area, the inspector must be able to use their professional judgement to consider the ages, development, and stages of the children in your setting.

So, think about what you expect from a child in your setting when they are having an outburst. Think about their age and whether you are expecting too much from them to understand why they are not happy. Think about what you can put in place to encourage children to self-regulate.

Within the Statutory Framework for the Early Years Foundation Stage (2021), it is clearly documented:

3.54. 'Providers must not give or threaten corporal punishment to a child and must not use or threaten any punishment which could adversely affect a child's well-being.

Providers must take all reasonable steps to ensure that corporal punishment is not given by any person who cares for or is in regular contact with a child, or by any person living or working in the premises where care is provided. Any Early Years provider who fails to meet these requirements commits an offence. A person will not be taken to have used corporal punishment (and therefore will not have committed an offence), where physical intervention 57 was taken for the purposes of averting immediate danger of personal injury to any person (including the child) or to manage a child's behaviour if absolutely necessary.

Providers, including childminders, must keep a record of any occasion where physical intervention is used, and parents and/or carers must be informed on the same day, or as soon as reasonably practicable.'

Writing a behaviour policy is one of the key points, in terms of ensuring consistency when relaying boundaries with children.

There has been much debate about the word behaviour, and I have read many articles and attended several courses regarding how we need to encourage children to self-regulate. We can only do this if we as practitioners learn to co-regulate with children, and, in turn, help them become more resilient.

Think about strategies you have established to help children to learn to calm down. For example, making emotion tubes, using breathing techniques to stabilise their breathing rhythm which in turn creates a sense of calm. These are easy to make and when children are able to do this with you, they will then learn the purpose - remember the INTENT.

So, when writing such a policy, it needs to be made clear and concise for all staff members to follow. Be sure to include in your policy stipulations for inculcating in children self-regulation of their emotions and the reason and the different strategies employed. This will show the inspector you are fully aware of different stages of behaviour development and how you are able to engage all children with their self-regulation methods.

You need to ensure that the following points are covered:

- Children need to be able to access a caring, positive atmosphere and demonstrate the ability to self-discipline. They need to be kept safe from both physical and emotional harm.
- The expectation of children's behaviour needs to be high in embracing honesty and the need for good manners.
- For children to be able to achieve this, there needs to be mutual respect between practitioners and children as well as between staff. The relationships which are maintained need to promote a positive environment and children must have a clear understanding of what is and is not acceptable behaviour.
- Practitioners need to work with parents or carers to help improve the behaviour of children and endeavour to offer a non-confrontational solution when conflicts arise between children and practitioners. This will be provided by inculcating positive attitudes, establishing courtesy towards each other as well as practitioners and reinforcing the importance of parents as role models through being approachable and caring.
- It is good practice for each setting to have a nominated person named within the policy so that practitioners can voice their concerns. Why not call this Regulation Champion?

Your inspector will certainly want to see children behaving well. However, good behaviour does not mean that they all sit quietly at the table. We all know this is not possible and not a great way for children to learn and develop. They need to have the freedom to choose what they wish and be able to manage their own feelings with their peers.

We know that some children's behaviour can have a huge impact on our day itself; can you imagine how this impacts other children and also the child himself?

I have grown to love the challenge of identifying disruptive behaviour patterns within a setting and finding out the root cause of why it is happening. Children's emotional well-being is paramount and holds the key to the success of learning and development. And with the past couple of years, children have experienced one of the saddest childhood experiences by missing out on so much by not being able to socialise and meet up with friends and family.

If you haven't already check Adverse Childhood Experiences (ACE). Going through Covid-19 has recently amplified some ACEs with the increase of poverty and domestic violence in the home and this will impact children for the rest of their lives.

I need you all to be aware when reading this that negative behaviour can be a display of unmet basic needs. Your practitioners will be the first to identify any adverse behaviour in the children, as they are their key person. Find out why the child is behaving this way and help find a solution. The child is a tiny acorn and will not turn into a proud oak tree without the support of watering and nurturing along its journey.

On occasions, some signs of undesirable behaviour may be a cause for concern and this is abuse (and I am not saying this is true in all cases, but any untoward behaviour must be documented and acknowledged). It is your duty of care and part of the reporting requirement for you to recognise signs of any significant changes of behaviour and record/report them, if necessary, following your local area guidance.

I am a qualified safeguarding instructor and when delivering training I offer the cause for concern form to our delegates. If this is something you wish to have a look at also and compare to yours then please visit the website.

www.jigsawearlyyearsconsultancy.com/are-you-ready-for-your-inspection-book-downloads/

The password is #AUR3-2022

Another reason which may cause unwanted behaviour is that your expectations of what the child can do may be unrealistic (too high or too plain), for their age and stage of development. This is why it is extremely important for practitioners to have a sound knowledge of child development to ensure that their expectations are not wrong for the children in your setting.

Once practitioners have this knowledge, this expectation, it needs to be communicated in an appropriate and easily comprehensible way for the child to understand. It also needs to be consistent. Remember, Rome was not built in a day and a child has taken months to get to this stage of behaviour - so expecting them to change in a week is highly unreasonable. And having any unrealistic expectations of an overnight reform will only make you, your team and the children anxious. Ensure that you keep parents involved in the strategies you have chosen as your inspector will want to see and hear how effectively you involve all those who are needed to make sure that the children's needs are holistically met.

Think about the environment you have provided to the children.

Points which you may want to consider:

- Is the area too big for children?
- Is there any way you can create quiet spaces for children - if they need to self-regulate?
- Is there a mix of children that causes the child to behave in this way?
- Can you create areas and group time that enables the child to learn and develop without becoming angry or anxious to prevent unwanted behaviour?
- Is the space in your setting too visually stimulating?
- Are there too many activities out for children that they cannot decide?
- Are there not enough stimulating activities for children so they appear bored?

This is important and research evidences that a vast array of colours can overstimulate a child's brain and cause behavioural issues. Here, first, you should rule out any issues of safeguarding concerns and ensure that the environment is suitable for a child to learn. Now, the next step would be to identify whether a child needs any additional support through outside agencies. This can impact a child's behaviour as they are not able to comprehend how to calm themselves or communicate effectively. Think about whether a child is having a transition at home which may also have an impact on this; for example, a new baby, parents' divorce, limited language skills, or even the overuse of a digital source such as a tablet.

Once every avenue has been thoroughly investigated and researched, only then initiate implementing the self-regulation strategies for the child. Your inspector will want to see what strategies you have in place for any behavioural issues and how effectively this has helped the child. In addition, use this time to show your observations where you may be able to assess what triggers this unwanted behaviour. Make sure you evaluate this and ensure that you explain what you are doing next to help the child's behaviour.

How do you include parents/carers, outside agencies, key person and the child on an everyday basis? Your inspector may want to talk to the parents of children you have concerns with to see whether you are sharing this information and if they feel content with the strategies you have in place.

Biting

One common incident in an Early Years setting is biting. This can cause friction between parents and staff, the child who has been bitten and for the biter themselves. This can also quite often be a cause for an escalation or a complaint.

Think about whether you have instated a separate Biting Policy or if this is included in your Positive Behaviour Policy. Your inspector will want to see this policy to make sure that you are following the defined procedure. This is the purpose of your policies and procedures. What you write in this is what you need to follow!

Do remember that children bite for a reason. Again, you have to find out why. While you try to understand this behaviour, please note that children do not understand why they feel the need to bite. They do not understand how this can hurt others.

Biting is a form of exploration of their environment, especially with young children. Think about whether they are hungry and thirsty as this could perhaps be their way of communicating to you - as they are unable to relay this information any other way.

Some children bite because they are teething or because they want your attention. If this is the case, turn your attention to the child who has been bitten as they need it more at that time. Children who have communication and language difficulties sometimes bite to get themselves heard.

I know I hear you say they are certainly doing that! If this is happening, think about outside agencies that can help you with encouraging children to communicate such as visual cards or sign language. One setting I visited during my travels had a 'time-out area', where children went to sit and 'calm down' when displaying unwanted behaviour.

It got to the point where children took themselves to this place in order to calm down, a behaviour they learnt. Think about the impact this has on the child in this area. Is this really an appropriate strategy to use to help children to display positive behaviour? I am hoping you are saying it isn't!

The word sorry!

There has been much debate about encouraging young children to say sorry. Commonly, it is believed, this could have the opposite effect of what you are trying to achieve (i.e. kindness) and will lead children to not develop a proper understanding and become less kind and caring.

This is hard as we are brought up in a nation of saying sorry for the simplest of things and it comes as easy as the drop of a hat. Think about it, as a nation do we say sorry for the slightest of things and is that only lip-service or do we really feel sorry?

In your setting, you will encounter many incidents involving a victim and an abuser. Try and encourage children to realise what they have done, when they have displayed this behaviour and how it makes the other child/person feel.

As a practitioner, talk to the child who is the victim and explain to them that you are sorry that another child has hurt them. This turns your attention away from the perpetrator and turns your focus to the other child. This will encourage children to develop empathy skills; eventually, the child will start to display how sorry they really are.

If this is the way you encourage children in your setting, make sure you put this in your Positive Behaviour Policy and explain the reason to the inspector. They will want to know the impact of your decision in your setting. Again, the word IMPACT comes into play.

You need to provide clear guidance to your inspector on the children's understanding of, 'What is acceptable behaviour'. And, if you have older children, for example, in an afterschool club, it is a good idea to encourage children to create their own behaviour contract.

I have seen this in several afterschool clubs. Not only does it give older children a sense of autonomy, but it also gives them a sense of self-worth that they are being listened to. When your inspector arrives in your afterschool setting, encourage children to interact with the inspector and explain how they put the contract and rules together. This is highly effective and also covers British Values given that children have a voice and are able to give opinions.

Under this judgement, the inspector will want to see if the children have high levels of respect for each other. And assess, if they are able to show they are confident learners and demonstrate an understanding of rules regarding behaviour.

Patience and independent thinking

Have you ever been in a setting where a child has explained to another child that they need to share and they are going to watch the sand timer - when it finally reaches the bottom of the glass then it is their turn. This is just perfect and would be ideal if we could encourage this in every setting.

The ideal scenario is when the children are able to make those right choices to enable learning to take place. Here, they demonstrate high self-control and when they are struggling they persevere. We step in far too quickly sometimes when they are struggling, especially if we are in a rush. Think about this when children are going outside, or getting ready for snack or lunch time. Try to stop and watch what happens when a child is trying to do up their zip, place their right feet into their wellington boots, wash their hands, and turn the tap on. These moments are just perfect to encourage independent skills and children should be able to take pride in what they have achieved.

Children need to be able to listen well and have high levels of concentration. They should be equipped with the necessary skills to use their curiosity to learn through their play. They should be able to listen to instructions and use these to become motivated learners who want to engage more. This enables children to become safe and secure in their surroundings.

If children's behaviour is poor within your setting this shows that learning will be poor. We need to be aware that if children are not engaged and actively involved in their activities, this can lead to poor behaviour. This, in turn, will hinder children's learning not only for themselves but for others. If this is the case, be mindful this would lead to an inadequate grade for the setting on inspection.

Confidence

We all know that children need to be able to be confident learners, be very self-aware and understand whether they are successful or not in their learning achievements. Inspectors will want to see how children bounce back from their less-than-perfect results if needed, and how they are able to become resilient to adverse outcomes.

Through life's challenges, children need to be able to come back and thrive through the numerous strengths they have developed with the aid of their key person. We have an innate drive regarding the capacity of resilience; however, this does have to be worked upon not only in our lives but the lives of children.

We need to be able to encourage resilience with children as early as possible, be the role models that children desire us to be and ensure that we are building and encouraging children's confidence at all levels of their learning and development.

Your inspector will want to see that children are able to be independent and have the ability to explore, think for themselves by themselves and use their imagination. Using the basis of Characteristics of Effective Learning will help children prepare for their transitions within your own setting, whether this pertains from room to room or during the reception year at school.

In this section children need to be able to demonstrate their positive attitudes through their curiosity and their high levels of engagement as well as their resilience. They need to be able to listen and respond positively to you and each other.

Children need to take pride in what they have achieved.

Take a look at your children in your setting. Do they do this?

How can you encourage more resilience and a sense of pride in what they have achieved?

8

PERSONAL DEVELOPMENT

The next reporting judgement is *Personal Development*.

Inspectors will evaluate the extent to which your setting is successfully promoting children's personal development. They will use their own professional judgement to consider how effective your setting is in regards to the children's all-round development. They will ensure whether or not the setting is mindful of the ages and stages of development of each child.

Evidence of planning within the area of children's personal, social and emotional development will be used to see how you are able to supplement the inspector's observations.

The impact of their findings will secure your grading in this area and other pieces of evidence are likely to include:

- Evidence of how children's well-being is assessed.
- Discussions with key persons, children, and parents regarding the key person system and their effective use.

- What experiences children are being given to provide a sense of understanding surrounding our families, as well as communities different to our own.

Practitioners must be able to teach children how to express themselves and share their emotions in a way that is appropriate.

Take the time to reflect upon this in your setting.

How do you ensure that children are confident enough to manage these transitions?

Write down the transitions of your children with your staff team.

These transitions are accompanied by emotional security and attachments for the practitioners. Attachments with key persons need to be robust to ensure that children are confident within their own development and are ready to explore their new surroundings and environment.

Again, take the time to talk to your staff and ask them how extensively they know their key children.

This is so important.

Ask questions such as what the children's likes and dislikes are:

- What are they interested in at present and how is this being cultivated and developed?
- Are they able to autonomously evolve their self-learning?
- Do they have a schema and how is this knowledge being used to increase their life skills and improve on their own development?

- Do children feel safe with their peers and show mutual respect?

If questions like these are answered well, you can safely say that your key staff members know their key children and this earns them a substantial credit.

Key person

Children succeed and thrive from a foundation of secure, warm, and loving care provided by the key people in their lives. During the day, we as practitioners become that person by taking on the role of the main carer - providing the stability, support, and comfort to the children. The key person is required to get to know the child's personality well so that they can understand and meet their specific needs.

Think about how you choose the key person for a child:

- Do you wait until a child builds up relationships with an adult when they first start at the setting?
- Do you encourage home visits with an allocated key person, to arrange a meeting with the child alongside the parents and initiate and build on the attachment from the start?
- Or is the key person chosen because they only have seven key children and all the other staff members have eight?

Whichever way you choose the key person, pause and think about the impact this will have on the child. Why are you following this particular selection method and how can you improve? We know we can all improve, but ensuring that we are continually striving to develop our own skills will guarantee that we are a reflective setting.

With this in mind, do you have a Key Person Policy? Do all staff members know the reason they have been assigned the role of a key person, or is it something you always have done on an auto-mode?

Do you have a key person buddy system for when the key person is not in the setting? If so, brilliant, this shows you are ensuring children's needs are being met. If not, introduce this now to ensure consistency in the quality of care in your setting.

Why not think about using one as part of your induction programme so that all staff members are aware of the underpinning reasons?

The key person must be able to provide the following for a child:

- Close attachment
- Familiarity
- Supported learning
- Comfort
- Encouragement
- Learning opportunities
- Consistent boundaries

Your inspector will want to see what support each key person gives their key children.

Things to remember:

- How many key children should be assigned to one key

person, to effectively ensure a good partnership with each child?
- Does the key person support each of their key children to become familiar with the setting and to feel confident and safe within it?
- Is the key person the practitioner who provides maximally possible comfort and care for their key child?
- Does each key person develop a genuine bond with each child and their parents - supporting children to form secure relationships?

Fundamental British Values

Under this area, children's personal development will be monitored, in the context of how well prepared they are as regards a wider society and life in Britain. This means that fundamental British Values will need to be evidenced to show their impact on children. This, however, **does not mean a display board.** This is not what your inspector wants to see in practice. They will want to see how children are able to understand the fundamental rules within your setting. Are they involved in making these rules?

I have seen many settings that are able to exemplify British Values in their everyday practice and here are just some examples.

Rule of law

Children in an afterschool club are able to create their own rules. As an activity, they use this time to discuss what they want to follow in their setting and create a poster to remind all children that the rules were *made by children for children*. This activity evidenced an impact that was huge as it gave children the autonomy, self-confidence and self-worth in helping boost their self-esteem.

A preschool that I visited a few years ago used superhero characters as their rules. For example, at a child's height, they had placed several of these as reminders to themselves of what is right or wrong. Superman was used as a reminder to use their walking feet. Similarly, Snow White was a reminder to be polite by saying please and thank you, and Spiderman was used to portray to be kind with our hands.

I observed children reminding each other of these characters. For example, when running, one child pointed his friend to Superman and recapped the need to walk. This was a delight to see and is a great example of the rules made by children for children ethos.

Mutual respect and tolerance

Mutual respect and tolerance for others are about learning to understand and appreciate each other's differences without allowing those differences to cause a change in the treatment of any sort. It is about being a cohesive part of a diverse community where not everyone is the same and forming relationships within that without discrimination.

Think about how you promote this conformity with diversity in your setting. Naturally, we are promoting inclusivity where we value different faiths and cultures, but how do we explore these fully, in order to ensure that we encourage children to recognise differences and similarities and exchange ideas irrespective of individual ethnicity.

Again, your inspector does not want to see the obligatory display board with people all around the world. Think about what impact this has on children's learning. Think about the everyday practice and how you encourage children to tolerate and thrive with each other. Children need to be given a wide range of opportunities to be able to practice tolerance and challenge any stereotypical behaviour that may occur. Children also need to be able to share ideas and stories that really value their diverse experiences and encourage them to learn from each other.

Individual liberty

In addition to being confident, through learning self-awareness, children need to have a positive sense of themselves. You can provide opportunities for children to develop this and increase their confidence in their own abilities. Enable children to have a voice and take risks, talk about their own experiences, explore their own feelings, reflect on their differences and concurrently value other children's opinions.

Having the chance to share how they are feeling when they are preparing for the transition to school, is one observation I was able to make in a preschool I inspected. They used the small group time to prepare children for the next stage of their learning. Herein, they were able to listen and used the loose parts table for children to illustrate how they were feeling by looking in a mirror and creating their emotions on the wood slice.

Practitioners were able to talk to children about what they would be feeling when they started Year R. In fact, they refrained from calling it 'Big School' as they felt this would create anxiety among children. Instead, with the use of words with positive connotations, they wanted to encourage the children's confidence for the next stage of their lives. The impact was indeed thought-provoking within this setting as children were given a voice and were being heard. They relished in their key person engaging in conversation with them, and you could see that children were very confident and excited about the next phase of their journey.

Democracy

As part of democracy in British Values, children need to be able to have a vote. This links to personal, social and emotional development; and the practitioners need to encourage children to know their own perspectives, value each other's views and make decisions as a collective force. An idea would be to encourage children to vote on which activity they liked best during the day. Children should be given adequate opportunities to develop their curious minds, in an environment where their questions are valued.

I believe that children's emotional well-being does affect their behaviour and welfare. Get this right and certainly, children will be in the right place to learn effectively. This is so important. We sometimes forget that children have feelings and the things we do to ensure they are learning can be reduced to a tick box exercise.

To remember use this acronym (**DRIM**)

Democracy

Rule of Law

Individual Liberty

Mutual Respect and Tolerance

. . .

Take this time to reflect on your setting and think about the last time you just listened to a child's conversation, their worries and successes without recording it somewhere.

Keeping children healthy

Ask yourself and your staff how they and the children keep themselves healthy. In fact, the topic constitutes an imperative agenda for the staff meeting exercise. As when asked this question by the inspector, practitioners can often freeze and struggle to explain themselves.

Part of the reporting requirements is to explain to your inspector how you keep the children physically active. Do your staff members know how many minutes of the day children need to be active?

With 1 in 10 children not meeting the minimum required amount of being physically active each day, the Department of Health campaign aims for children to be moving and promoting physical activity for at least 180 minutes per day. This can be recognised as tummy play in the babies to being able to walk unaided as they grow from toddlers to children at the age of five as not sitting for long periods of time.

Many of the settings where I have visited had taken away the chairs and used small quiet spaces for children to use when they needed to rest. This impact shows that children are active when they are standing at a table doing an activity. Take this time to reflect upon how much 'sitting down' a child does in your setting and how can you show that you are encouraging them to be physically active.

Think about the snacks children are able to have.

Do children have a choice and is the choice wide-ranging? Do you speak to children about healthy food and encourage this from an early age?

One setting I visited created a lovely activity at their 'coming together' time, which is widely referred to as circle time.

Children were asked to sit down in a circle and two trays and a basket of snacks were kept in the middle. I, along with the manager of the setting, was observing this activity.

The purpose was - is the snack a want or a need?

Lots of thought-provoking questioning was used to extend children's understanding of why we need certain foods. Children delighted in sharing how it would make them big and strong. Practitioners explained the difference between a want and a need to the children. Children encouraged each other and shared their points of view about the want for a biscuit - but the need for a banana.

Personal self-help skills

Encouraging children to be healthy is high on Ofsted's agenda and you will need to be able to demonstrate this to your inspector. Think about how you support children to be independent throughout their time in your setting.

There are several ways to do this, from toilet habits to encouraging children to wash their hands and even the simplest of things such as blowing nose.

- If you see a child who needs their nose wiped, what do you do?

- Do you get a tissue and wipe their nose for them?
- Do you ask them to find the tissue box and collect a tissue?
- Or do you have a nose-blowing station where children are able to do this for themselves and see what they are doing?

I have seen this in several settings now and highly recommend it being placed in all rooms from the toddlers to preschool.

Nose Blowing Station: Set aside an area, where there is an acrylic mirror on the walk, with words to the effect of: *Does your nose need blowing?* The sign should be in bold print for children to see clearly. In addition, a mirror is placed on a table that has a box of tissues which are replenished as soon as they are finished, along with a bowl of soapy water and hand towels. Encourage children to look in the mirror and explain to them about keeping their noses clean and washing their hands after doing so. One setting I visited were concerned that children would use the same water to wash their hands. I would recommend changing the water every few hours, but nowhere in the statutory framework is this stated as an unhealthy practice.

'Children acquire a strong sense of emotional well-being. They are great risk assessors and show self-control in a range of situations. For example, when being 'builders' children are aware of the need to wear safety goggles. Children have access to a wealth of interesting and innovative resources and play experiences that greatly support their interests. For example, children use magnets to investigate which objects are metal and they share their findings with others. Children relish their time as the 'responsible' helper. They confidently take orders from their friends and help to serve them healthy snacks.'

Compton and Shawford Preschool

This is an excellent way of encouraging children to be independent with their self-help skills.

Within this section of personal development as practitioners, we need to *'help children to gain an effective understanding of when they may be at risk, including when using the internet, digital technology and social media and where to get support if they need it.'*

Children should be made aware that they need to keep themselves safe. How do you ensure this awareness as well as the implementation of this safety?

There has been much discussion regarding the number of times children are engaged in screen time. If children are unable to access the internet in your setting think about how you help parents understand the importance of their children using the internet. We need to be raising awareness of how important it is to know what children are looking at when they are online.

We need to be giving clear consistent messages to children that support healthy choices around their health and well-being.

Through conversation or encouraging the children to talk about the risks within the setting? Another outstanding example is encouraging children to risk assess themselves with their own risk assessment sheets, which they create themselves. By provoking an engaging conversation about whether something is safe or not can help a child to think like this on an everyday basis.

Encourage the responsible helper to use their own forms, where they are able to mark the score using a tick sheet or tally the resources and activities. Not only does this give a child a sense of pride and well-being, but it also gives them the power to use and apply their brains for risk, prevention, and correction which in turn helps them in making decisions and being resilient.

You must also make sure that you have the following as part of the welfare requirements

'Where food and snacks and drinks are provided they must be healthy, balanced and nutritious' How do you ensure what you provide comprises of all these things?

Think about children's lunchboxes: How do you ensure these are healthy?

The time to actually talk about what is expected from parents is when they visit with their child at the very beginning, especially with regards to the lunch boxes. Talk about how there may be allergies within the setting and you need to make sure that children are kept safe from any unwanted goodies (which is a want, not a need) such as crisps, chocolate, and sweets.

Fresh drinking water must be available at all times - how do you do this? Please be mindful that if children have their own water bottles, they only access this as opposed to just taking any random bottle at any time. Stomach bugs can spread all too quickly and the children need to be monitored constantly to prevent any such infection.

There must be an area that is adequately equipped to provide healthy snacks and drinks. Include suitable hygienic preparation of food and drink for children.

How do you ensure that the areas where you prepare bottles and food are constantly cleaned? Do you document this?

For this safety, just a handful of the welfare requirements need to be abided by, to ensure a risk-free environment. *See the Statutory Requirements of the Early Years Foundation Stage for the full version.*

Oral health

Oral health has been recognised that it needs to become a habit for children at the earliest stage hence why it has been added. The statistics say that nearly a quarter of five-year-olds in England have tooth decay and this is increasing. Having a tooth extracted is one of the most common procedures for children under six.

It is up to you and your setting how you promote oral health, you can link this to conversations about being healthy and healthy eating when you have good conversations with children at the snack or lunch table.

The guidance does not state that children need to be cleaning their teeth in your setting. In fact, I do wonder how this is risk assessed to stop cross-contamination. So use dolls, soft toys, read stories and share smiles, these are ways that can be used on an everyday basis to ensure that oral health is being talked about. Another good idea is to give parents an oral health sheet which helps them when children are at home and links to a partnership with parents and carers really well.

We have placed an oral health poster for parents on our website if you wish to download it.

www.jigsawearlyyearsconsultancy.com/are-you-ready-for-your-inspection-book-downloads/

The password is #AUR3-2022

For more information check out. www.gov.uk/government/publications/health-matters-child-dental-health

Diversity

Think about how you ensure that children know about similarities and differences between themselves and others amongst families, faiths, communities, cultures, and traditions?

When I asked these questions during my Quality Improvement visits as well as Early Years inspections, I often heard the reply, 'Well, we have a Polish little boy and we ask his parents for words to help him understand and we invite them in to talk to the children.' Another classic example is, 'We celebrate Chinese New Year and do a Food Tasting.'

No disrespect to these activities, which you are providing for the children, but think about when a child leaves your setting. What cultures are they able to see and relate with, in the outside world? Are they able to identify any other cultures or faiths? Ensure that you are able to demonstrate to your inspector that you encourage children to be aware of the cultures and faiths outside their own. This all comes under the umbrella of mutual respect and tolerance and should be demonstrated in your setting.

Consider the kind of impact this has on children's lives and how we can start encouraging children to be asking questions about how other people live from all around the world.

Think about your INTENT, IMPLEMENTATION, AND IMPACT!

We also need to be thinking about how we promote diversity in our setting. How do we talk to children about our differences and what makes us unique?

Some ideas may help you here:

- Provide experiences that enable children to develop positive individual and group identities. Encourage children to appreciate their own culture, race and language backgrounds so they can then appreciate other backgrounds too.
- Use visual aids that represent people from diverse backgrounds. Although do not use these as a token. They need to be promoted in a way that provokes conversation.
- Celebrate the fact we are all different and enable children to share their experiences by listening to their voices.
- Encourage a family wall at their height. Encourage children to talk to their friends and their family.
- When children ask questions, answer them truthfully and talk about their ideas and observations.
- Provide opportunities for children to interact with people from a wide range of racial, cultural and linguistic backgrounds. Ask family and friends to visit.

One setting I visited had a storyteller who read amazing stories to the children. He was a Rastafarian from Jamaica and children were mesmerised by his hair. He used this in his stories and the children asked questions which staff answered regarding the differences between us. This provoked a brilliant activity surrounding 'this is me'.

So think of ideas that you can do that can provoke conversations surrounding all of our different backgrounds and remember to talk about being kind.

Welfare

How are the children keeping themselves safe? Does this include their safety against the abuse of the internet and social media?

This may not be suitable for your Early Years setting, but if you are a childminder or afterschool club, how do you ensure children are keeping themselves safe? Also, what documentation and safety measures do you have in place to protect the children?

Overall quality and effectiveness of your provision.

Your inspector will want to be able to evaluate your quality, and it is up to you to ensure that they are able to see this by being consistent, transparent and clear in your delivery of Early Years.

Specifically, the inspectors will evaluate and report on:

- How well your setting meets the needs of the range of children who attend.
- How well practitioners know their key children and where they are in their learning from their starting points to the next stage of their education.
- How well is the curriculum (EYFS) planned, designed and implemented?
- The contribution of your setting to children's well-being and whether they are emotionally safe, secure and happy.
- The effectiveness of leadership and management of your setting especially in the evaluation on how to improve.

So remember

What is your INTENT?

How are you going to IMPLEMENT this?

What is the IMPACT?

9

LEADERSHIP AND MANAGEMENT

Leadership and management assume great importance in the Early Years settings. To be a good leader, you need to shine from the top and ensure your team is aligned with you to take the journey with you.

'We must be the change we wish to see in the world.'

Mahatma Gandhi

Without your team being a part of your ethos, you will struggle to achieve as much as you want to. The inspector will want to assess and evaluate the effectiveness of your leadership and management in terms of subsequent impacts on your setting. This chapter will break down the areas that must be demonstrated/described and give examples of what you can showcase.

Judgement of leadership and management

There are several questions that you need to ask yourself so that you are confident in your answers.

These answers will facilitate the judgement of leadership and management by evaluating the level of the following:

- How do you demonstrate the vision of your setting? Do you have high expectations of what the children in your setting can achieve and ensure that you have corresponding high standards of care for the children?
- How do you improve your staff's practice of teaching and learning and provide effective levels of supervision to ensure that you are promoting appropriate professionalism?
- How do you evaluate the quality of your setting and ensure that the accounts of the staff, children, and parents are taken into consideration to ensure progressive improvement?
- How do you implement learning programmes and a sequenced curriculum that meets the relevant statutory requirements during the Early Years Foundation stage, whilst also considering and addressing the issues relevant to the children's interests?
- How do you successfully plan and manage the curriculum/learning programmes so that children get a good start in their learning journey and are well prepared for the next stage of their learning as well as the bigger picture before being ready for school?
- How do you record the IMPACT of what you implement?

- How do you constantly promote equality and diversity ensuring that British Values are demonstrated and that poor behaviour towards others is acted upon? Here, the term poor behaviour needs to include bullying and discrimination. The required learning outcomes of different groups of children also need to be demonstrated and accordingly met.
- How do you make sure that you meet all the statutory and other government requirements regarding the protection of children, promoting their welfare and are alongside able to prevent radicalisation and extremism?
- How do you ensure that all children, irrespective of their background are ready for their next stage of learning? How do you ensure that each child experiences the awe and wonder of the world and is ably equipped to apply those experiences to prepare them for school?

Considering the following guidelines, we will break down each section, specify what this means and how you can ensure that you are meeting the needs of the requirements with impact.

Safeguarding

One of the reporting criteria at which an inspector will take a close look is: 'How effective is your safeguarding within your setting?' The aim is to ensure a thriving and safe and secure environment for the children in your setting. They will consider how well the leaders and managers have created a culture of vigilance where children's welfare is accorded the top priority. In addition, they will also evaluate in case there are any concerns and that these are acted upon swiftly.

Safeguarding covers a huge spectrum of parameters, which not only come under the Leadership and Management area but also includes personal development. So, if you have a safeguarding concern at your inspection, please be aware that this will impact both judgements in these areas.

Settings will need to consider the Working Together to Safeguard Children (2018) and Information Sharing for Practitioners (2018); in this reference, please note the date as the new versions should be used. In addition to these, Prevent Duty also need to be digested and used within your own safeguarding policy. Please also consider the 'Inspecting Safeguarding in Early Years, Education and Skills settings', Ofsted 2019. This guidance gives you the core information regarding the expected range of evidence required by an inspector on the inspection day. This guidance should be read in the context of the Early Years Inspection Handbook 2019.

Five main aspects of safeguarding

The inspectors investigate five main aspects under the safeguarding remit. These include:

- How leaders, managers, and providers (this includes a committee) ensure a positive **culture** and ethos, to ensure these become an important part of everyday life within a setting. This also includes all levels of training in safeguarding, at every level.
- The effectiveness of the safeguarding policies includes safer recruitment and vetting processes. In addition, the staff should be able to recognise and identify the signs when children may be at harm

either within the setting or in the family or wider community outside the setting.
- The quality of the safeguarding practice should entail the functionality that staff is aware of the types and signs of abuse whilst ensuring that the welfare of all children is kept at the forefront.
- The response time, if any safeguarding concerns are raised, should also be factored in devising the safeguarding framework. This is so important and often compliant visits are raised because concerns were not actioned quick enough or directed to the right organisation.
- The quality of support when working with multi-agencies around a plan for a child.

Inspectors will need to consider how you, in the capacity of a leader or manager, has instated the following arrangements under the listed headings:

IDENTIFY children who may need any early help or are at risk of neglect, abuse, grooming, and exploitation.

HELP prevent abuse by raising awareness among children of any safeguarding risks and who and where to get help in order to support them when needed.

HELP those children who are at risk of abuse and need Early Years help or statutory social care involvement, keep accurate records, and ensure timely referrals. In addition, it is essential to have working liaisons with other agencies to ensure that children get the help and support they need.

Also, to be able to **MANAGE** allegations about adults who may be a risk, and check the suitability of staff who work with children.

We will cover each section and explain what needs to be evidenced throughout the course of your practice.

Firstly, how does the committee, leader or yourself, if a childminder, ensure a safeguarding culture and ethos is promoted through everyday practice.

Inspectors will want to see the following:

- Policies that have been reviewed regularly and demonstrate the incorporation of new legislation/documentation: Have they been updated with the new Working Together to Safeguard Children (2018). Please ensure you check this.
- Staff members are supported to develop an awareness of signs that a child may have been neglected or abused and have knowledge of 'What to do if you're worried a child is being abused.'
- All staff members, leaders, committee members and volunteers must receive appropriate safeguarding training, which needs to be updated regularly. It is pertinent that all are aware of their responsibilities regarding how to protect children from harm.

There needs to be a Designated Safeguarding Lead (DSL) in charge of safeguarding with the appropriate level of training who fully understands that it is their responsibility to ensure all children are kept safe, all staff members are up-to-date with their training and remain confident in the knowledge to recognise any concerns.

The Statutory Framework for the Early Years Foundation Stage effective from 3rd April 2017 states under Section 3:

3.2. *'Providers must take all necessary steps to keep children safe and well. The requirements in this section explain what Early Years providers must do to: safeguard children; ensure the suitability of adults who have contact with children; promote good health; manage behaviour; and maintain records, policies and procedures.'*

As well as:

3.5. *'A practitioner must be designated to take lead responsibility for safeguarding children in every setting.*

Childminders must take the lead responsibility themselves. *The lead practitioner is responsible for liaising with local statutory children's services agencies, and with the LSCB. They must provide support, advice, and guidance to any other staff on an ongoing basis, and any specific safeguarding issue as required. The lead practitioner must attend a child protection training course that enables them to identify, understand and respond appropriately to signs of possible abuse and neglect'*

Operating in the capacity of a childminder, you are the DSL and hence, must take on the responsibility yourself. You need to ensure that your training is suitable to meet the needs of the safeguarding of children in your setting.

The inspector will want to speak to the DSL to ensure that the Lead is confident in the referral process of any safeguarding concerns. When asked questions, the designated personnel should know the process confidently, be thorough in their knowledge of the setting's safeguarding policy and ensure that they give the inspector enough confidence that they know the mandated procedure in case of any untoward incidents.

In case any referrals have been made, the inspector will want to check whether this was shared with the local authority, in conjunction with timely written secured records. You do have 48 hours to share the information, but as a qualified safeguarding instructor, I can say that it is paramount to get those forms to the correct agency as quickly as possible. Your policy also needs to state the time limit within which you need to have all the documentation sent to the correct agencies.

Your inspector will also check for any safeguarding incidents or allegations since the last inspection and whether these have been resolved or are ongoing. These will, in all probability, be checked as early in the inspection as possible as it will impact your judgement as regards your effectiveness of safeguarding.

Settings must also be risk assessed and this needs to be demonstrated to your inspector. You have to protect babies and children and ensure that age-appropriate, reasonable risks form an adequate part of their development.

When it comes to safeguarding children, the Framework (2017) confirms:

4. *'Providers must have and implement a policy and procedures to safeguard children.'*

This policy will be asked for during your inspection, including several others. These will be checked and clarified to ensure your compliance and adherence to what is stated in your policy. If you are not following your own policy, this could, in fact, lead to an *inadequate* grading.

Regarding Child Protection, the framework affirms the following:

'These should be in line with the guidance and procedures of the relevant Local Safeguarding Children Board (LSCB). The safeguarding policy and procedures must include an explanation of the action to be taken when there are safeguarding concerns about a child and in the event of an allegation being made against a member of staff, and cover the use of mobile phones and cameras in the setting.'

You will also be aware of smart devices that staff are now wearing. Is it appropriate for staff to wear these, do they need to and what procedures do you have in place to protect children from the use of them?

Have you considered these in your policies?

If not please ensure you do. A smartwatch will have a lens to take pictures and these are easily able to download from.

So, for example, a staff member could position their phone somewhere with a clear view of the nappy changing area and remotely access the phone's camera on their smartwatch from somewhere else in or outside the nursery. They would have the ability to zoom in using the smartwatch and take multiple photos.

This will be something inspectors will be checking for in your policies as a line of enquiry. If staff are wearing these devices, what protection do you have in your setting for children? Make this an action to check today.

Please be mindful that as per the Working Together to Safeguard Children (2018) the Local Safeguarding Children Board has transitioned to Safeguarding Partners.

Your policy MUST follow your Safeguarding Partner's procedure to report any concerns as well as an allegation against a member of your staff. It is also recommended to allocate a time frame to do this in case you have a concern or a disclosure.

This is important, and inspectors will want to know that your Designated Safeguarding Lead is fully aware of what to do in case of unforeseen scenarios.

When writing your safeguarding policy, you will realise that it is extensive in terms of the influence. Here is a list of subheadings, which need to be covered. Remember, this needs to be bespoke to your setting:

1. List the types of safeguarding concerns that may arise in your setting.
2. How should you deal with these concerns?
3. What is the timeframe within which these concerns are to be informed to relevant authorities?
4. Who is the Designated Safeguarding Lead?
5. Details of recruitment and supervision of staff (this does include your assistants if you are a childminder).
6. How you create a safe environment?
7. How you record and store information in line with GDPR?
8. How will you respond to any complaints or allegations against staff?
9. Details of Prevent duty and FGM.
10. What are the regulations concerning the use of mobile phones and cameras?

11. What are the protocols for E-safety?

This list is not exhaustive but it does give you a fair idea on what to include.

Prevent duty and potential questions

The inspector will also focus on understanding and assessing the knowledge level of the staff regarding Prevent Duty and FGM.

As an ex-inspector, there were questions that I needed to ask and record as pieces of evidence to ensure that the staff members were aware of how to recognise any signs and report the same to the DSL.

Examples of potential questions include:

1. What does the Prevent Duty protect children from?
2. How would a childcare setting demonstrate that they are protecting children from being drawn into terrorism?
3. In what existing policies would you expect to read about the Prevent Duty?
4. If you suspected a child was being radicalised, to whom/which authorities would you report your concerns?
5. What signs would you look out for if you suspected a child was being radicalised?
6. Can you name all of the British Values that should be embedded into your practice and how do embed these into your everyday practice?

Vetting process

The staff as well as volunteers need to be carefully selected when joining your setting and should be vetted in accordance with the statutory requirements. This should be reflected in the protocols defined in your application and recruitment procedure. The inspector will also speak to staff in your setting to ensure that the stated procedure is being followed. Usually, conversations are initiated with the newest member of your team.

If you have assistants as a childminder, it is also important for you to show that they applied for the post using the defined channels and highlight the steps taken by you to ensure their suitability. This needs to be recorded as a process and for a demonstration to your inspector.

We have placed a safeguarding audit for you on our website to download and help you with this.

www.jigsawearlyyearsconsultancy.com/are-you-ready-for-your-inspection-book-downloads/

The password is #AUR3-2022

Working in partnership

> 'TEAM WORK
> *Coming together is a beginning*
> *Keeping together is progress*
> *'Working together is success'.*

Henry Ford

Working together in partnership with others is very high on the agenda during your inspection. How do you ensure that all parents feel they are being valued; they are interacting and engaging with their children's development and that you are listening to their voice? Also, how do you work with outside agencies to ensure that children's needs are being met?

The Early Years Foundation Stage (2021) states:

'The EYFS seeks to provide **partnership working** between practitioners and with parents and/or carers.'

If you can honestly say that you have all parents on board in your setting and that you are consistently working together to improve outcomes for children, this chapter is not for you.

However, I truly feel that we, as child educators, need to ensure we are engaging with all parents and carers and have strategies in place to make this happen.

Examples of the efficacy with which partnership is shown in an Ofsted report might look like this:

> "The childminder enthusiastically works with parents and shares ideas for home learning through home link books and activities. This actively encourages an excellent partnership with parents. She is excellent at communicating information with parents regarding their children's care, learning, and development.'
>
> **Nicola Facey, Childminder**

> 'Partnerships with parents are excellent. Information sharing between staff and parents is highly effective. The parent's

involvement in their child's learning ensures that children's needs are quickly identified and successfully met. Highly active links with the local schools and other settings create a tremendous sense of belonging for children and their families.'

Shawford and Compton Preschool, Winchester

These settings showed how their partnership with the parents was *outstanding*. They all knew their parents' needs and styles, which allowed them to help build the foundations of partnership. Parents' involvement was developed through a variety of methods in order to make it highly effective. They included the parents in the whole process of recruitment, thereby ensuring collaboration at its best.

Right from the time when a child first starts at your setting, you should inform parents of who their key person is. This is mandatory. The Statutory Framework of the Early Years Foundation (2021) states:

3.27 *'Each child **must** be assigned a key person. Their role is to help ensure that every child's care is tailored to meet their individual needs to help the child become familiar with the setting, offer a settled relationship for the child and build a relationship with their parents.'*

Think about what you do in your setting.

- Do you wait for a child to be given a key person?
- What makes you decide on the key person?
- As per the regulations, it is a 'must'.

Children need to build attachments to their key person who will subsequently ensure they are forming safe and secure relationships with their key child. In turn, this will give them the basis to know this child well enough and be ready to develop their learning through the environment.

2.1. *'Assessment plays an important part in helping parents, carers and practitioners to recognise children's progress, understand their needs, and to plan activities and support. Ongoing assessment (also known as formative assessment) is an integral part of the learning and development process. It involves practitioners*

knowing children's level of achievement and interests, and then shaping teaching and learning experiences for each child reflecting that knowledge. In their interactions with children, practitioners should respond to their own day-to-day observations about children's progress and observations that parents and carers share...'

How do you do this? Try answering the following questions:

- What method do you use to observe, assess and plan for a child? How do you ensure parents are involved in this process?
- Do you use an online tracking tool and give parents the login to see where their child is in the development cycle?
- How do you ensure parents understand how this works?
- Why not invite parents to an evening's training about how the online tool works and use this time to emphasise the importance of working in tandem whilst assessing their children?

I understand that it can be a time issue, with parents being so busy, but there is nothing worse than having this as a recommendation in your report when, in fact, something *could be done* about it.

Do your parents know that this is a reporting requirement and would affect your judgement grade? If not, LET them know. I am sure if they knew they would do everything they could to help you gain the rightful judgement during your inspection.

The Education Inspection Framework (Sept 2019 page 41) states:

'Leaders engage effectively with children, their parents and others in their community, including schools and other local services.'

I have inspected many settings. In my experience, when managers are asked the question about how they work in partnership with parents, they say they do their best to encourage this, but not all parents want to be involved in these conversations.

Firstly, when I would hear this, I would think that you are giving yourself a recommendation for your own report. So, before you start answering this question, think about all the ways in which you encourage parents to share their children's learning development. Please do not focus on parents who don't - think positively about all the parents who do focus and engage.

With this in mind, at Jigsaw Early Years Consultancy Ltd we have now created online training called 'The Parent Bundle'. So the purpose of this is to encourage settings to engage with all parents. As we can appreciate, time plays a huge part in working together. We have created a package, which you can purchase for parents when they start with you at your setting. This bundle has four online lessons which they can use on their own devices. Also, there are fact sheets and guidance on what to expect when their child starts at your setting. What better way to engage with those hard-to-reach parents and feel you are working together in partnership! This mechanism can have a huge impact on the way children learn and develop. If this is something which interests you to ensure engagement of all your parents, please email us on info@jigsaweyc.com with the subject of 'THE PARENT BUNDLE'.

Another question you may like to ask yourself: How do you work with other settings? Again, this is a reporting requirement and hence, will certainly be asked. It will also be followed up with seeking clarification from different staff members.

Think about how you do this? Do you send emails? Do you make phone calls? Do you share learning journals via your online tracking system? These channels adopted by you - do they work, is this two-way, interactive communication? If this does not work, why not?

What is your intention to improve on the communication between you and the other settings? How are you going to implement this and what is the subsequent impact on children's learning and development? Do you have any recorded evidence of this?

3 I's Formula

Consider this:

INTENT

IMPLEMENTATION

IMPACT

What better than using the 3 I's formula to demonstrate how you are evaluating your setting?

Going back to partnership with others, another 'faux pas' is to tell the inspector that you have tried to contact the other preschool, childminder, nursery but FAILED to get any response.

Do you recognise that in your setting? Have you tried all the possible strategies to engage with other settings? Can you honestly say that you have exhausted all options?

If you are not receiving any responses from other settings, why not give them a call and be honest with them. Explain that one of the reporting requirements within the statutory framework is to work with other settings and share development, strategies and needs of the child. Explain that as part of this process, you would like to work with them and explore the possibility of sending end-of-term reports to each other that can be used as a piece of evidence to show the inspector.

I cannot stress enough how important it is for settings to work together. In addition to being a *good* and *outstanding* practice, it shows you are according top priority to the child's needs.

So, think about outside agencies, and try and identify the agencies, using the following question: Do you know who you can work with and how to find out if you are able to receive help? This can be a mind-boggling question.

In many leadership and management discussions, the majority of managers and childminders, when asked this question, would say the same thing: *'We have tried to contact agencies but with limited funding, they are not able to help us'*. Sadly, we all know children's needs have to be met, however, we attribute our failure to the funding crisis. And this, in fact, may not be the case.

With the closure of children centres and the cutting off of your local council's funding, you may not be able to access the support you need. For example, for a child with behavioural concerns, do you have a Portage Service which can come out and support you? If the answer is no, have you thought about contacting the local Health Visitor as they may have a direct line, or may be able to help you by visiting and giving you some new strategies?

If you have concerns about a child's communication skills, are you able to contact the speech and language therapist of your local children's services and ask for some help? Quite often, the answer is, 'There's a waiting list.' In such cases, my advice would be not to delay in sourcing help. I am sure you will have kept records of observations, so when they do hopefully visit, they would be able to see that you have tried everything in your capacity to help that child to secure the required support. Again, please make sure parents are kept in the loop of association with other agencies.

There has to be a way of receiving additional help if needed and you as the settings leader or manager will need to find that way. Remember: Children's needs must come first.

Questions to consider when working in partnership

How do you ensure that your parents are happy? Such questions should start to provoke your thinking about what you do with your current set of parents? And, what is it that you can do to be in sync with the parents' understanding of happiness?

Do you use questionnaires and, if yes, how often do you send these out?

What do you do with that information and do you inform parents about the answers to the questions as a summary of your findings?

By doing so, you would help parents feel they are being listened to and are active participants in the development of their child. So when asked by your inspector whether their views are taken into consideration, their answer would be a confident YES.

What about a comment box? Do you use any such form or tool for encouraging parents to place their comments? How often do you look inside this box! Do remember that there is no point in providing a suggestion/comment box if you are not willing to act on the comments shared in the box. Also, you may be pleasantly surprised with some of these comments being positive feedback! How great would that be to share with your team, letting them know they feel valued?

Think about this:

Do you consider the views of outside agencies? Think about the ways you gather and collate information from outside agencies. Do you have a good rapport with them and how do you ensure congruity between your/their thought process whilst taking them seriously? This again assumes great importance for working with partners.

Do you record these details and again what do you do with this information and how do you show their impact on your setting?

Remember though that when you are sharing information with outside agencies, parents need to sign their consent, clarifying their agreement with this. This needs to be collected at the very outset when the children start with you.

Consider when they do not agree to sign the form. Do they have a valid reason for this? In case, parents do not agree to give their consent on the information sharing form, this also needs to be recorded.

Is this a cause for concern? And what are you going to do with this information?

Parents and carers need to be aware that if you have concerns about the well-being of their children, this becomes a 'duty of care' and you need to report this immediately regardless of whether they have signed the consent or not.

How well do you work with others to help you understand a child's development and ascertain ways of improving their learning? Think of the way you work with other settings childminders, preschools or nurseries to develop better insight into a child's development. How do you record this and show its impact on the child and your setting? Do you share children's Progress Check at 2 with the Health Visitor or do you only give a copy to parents? Think about if parents do not pass a copy of this very important document to the Health Visitor. With the absence of this information, some key points and concerns may not be communicated effectively. So my advice would be to share this with the Health Visitor as part of your ongoing partnership with outside agencies.

Have you considered encouraging parents to complete questionnaires to help you evaluate your practice? If not, why not?

For our example of a parent questionnaire please visit the website and download our template.

www.jigsawearlyyearsconsultancy.com/are-you-ready-for-your-inspection-book-downloads/

The password is #AUR3-2022

Examples of questions from the Ofsted inspector for parents

The Ofsted inspector may want to speak to a parent about the questionnaire and possibly ask a couple of questions to see how happy they are with your setting.

Examples of these inspector questions may include:

1. How long has your child been at the setting?
2. How often do they come to the setting?
3. What made you choose this setting for your child?
4. What was the initial, settling-in procedure like for you and your child?
5. Do you know where policies are kept and have you received a copy of the same?
6. Do you know who your child's key person is?
7. How often do you discuss your child's development?
8. What information is passed on during the pick-up times?
9. Do you know who to approach if you have any concerns?
10. In case you have any concerns about the manager or owner, who would you go to?

11. Did you know Ofsted has a complaint number you can call? The inspector will always direct parents to the Ofsted complaint number which needs to be displayed on the parents' notice board.
12. Would you recommend the setting to others and why?

In terms of achieving an *outstanding*, it is a good practice to ask parents questions about your setting especially because they are also your partners.

So why not give them a questionnaire to complete regularly. This will not only make them feel valued but will also help iron out any concerns which may arise and allow communication to run effectively. This will not only ensure achieving an *outstanding* practice but also the parents would be prepared for the questions on the day of inspection. Again, these questionnaires can be answered anonymously.

In addition to questionnaires for parents, why not give your staff time to answer a version also.

See our example of this.

www.jigsawearlyyearsconsultancy.com/are-you-ready-for-your-inspection-book-downloads/

The password is #AUR3-2022

Building on working in partnership with parents and staff and using the questionnaires to summarise your findings, consider doing the same for working in partnership with other settings. This also can be done anonymously, either by (i) sending out forms to the settings you work with or by (ii) creating a Google form where you can send the link and the responses will come through.

Examples of partnership questions

1. How long have you been working in partnership with the setting?
2. Do we work in partnership regularly?
3. Do you feel you are being listened to?
4. Do you know our safeguarding policy and procedure?
5. How does your setting provide relevant information about the needs of the children?
6. Does our setting value the contribution made by your organisation?
7. Does the setting share best practices and networking with others?
8. How does the setting work overall in partnership with yourselves?

Policies and procedures

A policy needs to ensure that it covers the beliefs and values of your setting and shows how you deliver best practice, including Early Years care and education. These are standards that can suitably guide you to be able to demonstrate a professional approach and continually deliver best practice.

They need to be easily comprehended by all staff members, parents, and carers. Your policies will inform your procedures and minimise risk for both children and staff within your setting. Your procedures take shape from your policies and specifically pertain to a series of actions that are carried out in a particular order.

Not only staff members but parents and carers also need to know about the nuances of your policies and procedures. This is not a pointless exercise merely to show off to the inspector during the inspection. Policies and procedures protect you, your setting and most importantly the children.

Inspectors will need to consider a sample of policies and these will include safeguarding and child protection, risk assessments, fire safety and any other policy that relates to health and safety, like the medicine policy and behaviour management policy.

Childminders are not required to have written policies and procedures. *However, they must be able to explain their policies and procedures to parents, carers, and others (for example Ofsted inspectors or the childminder agency with which they are registered) and ensure any assistants follow them.'*

A practice that achieves *good* to *outstanding* shows that childminders are fully aware of their policies and that these are documented, well-maintained in their folder or digitally and are bespoke to the childminder. I have been to many settings, including childminders, where they have thought it would be a better option to 'buy' the pre-written policies from the many sites.

Firstly, ask yourself this... Why?

Is it to save you the effort of writing them yourself? If so, when you use them, do you even understand what they mean? Consider if the wordings need to be customised and changed to make them right for you and your practice.

This is your setting, so make sure your policies are aligned to you and not written by or for anybody else. This not only helps you when you get inspected, as you can always refer to the policies written by you; it also helps you take ownership of your setting.

There is nothing worse for an inspector to see these pre-written policies with no changes to show that you haven't reflected upon each and taken ownership. You are only drawing negative attention to yourself, which will entail further questioning and investigation about what you know about your setting.

One of the most important policies will be your safeguarding policy and this will certainly be asked for during your inspection.

Health

The Statutory Framework of the Early Years Foundation Stage (2017) states:

'3.46. 'Providers must have and implement a policy, and procedures, for administering medicines. It must include systems for obtaining information about a child's needs for medicines, and for keeping this information up-to-date. Training must be

provided for staff where the administration of medicine requires medical or technical knowledge. Prescription medicines must not be administered unless they have been prescribed for a child by a doctor, dentist, nurse or pharmacist (medicines containing aspirin should only be given if prescribed by a doctor).'

Think about how you ensure that staff and parents are kept informed of your policies and procedures; when do you do this; and how often do you review your policies?

Complaints

The Statutory Framework of the Early Years Foundation Stage (2021) states:

3.75. *'Providers must put in place a written procedure for dealing with concerns and complaints from parents and/or carers, and must keep a written record of any complaints, and their outcome. Childminders are not required to have a written procedure for handling complaints, but they must keep a record of any complaints they receive and their outcome. All providers must investigate written complaints relating to their fulfilment of the EYFS requirements and notify complainants of the outcome of the investigation within 28 days of having received the complaint. The*

record of complaints must be made available to Ofsted or the relevant childminder agency on request.'

Your inspector will want to check your complaints folder to ensure that all complaints have been recorded and processed for resolution. Any complaints need to be reported to Ofsted for maintaining necessary records, regardless of how small it is. I cannot emphasise this point enough - doing so will help you show the inspector how professional you are in following your own policy.

Policy sharing

Firstly, staff should be aware of your policies through the robust processes implemented by you in the setting. For more information, read the earlier paragraph within this chapter. You need to ensure that staff members are kept up-to-date with any amendments being made to your policies.

As a previous group manager, in my personal experience, it was extremely difficult to guarantee that ALL staff members were aware and updated of these changes. One idea we had as an *outstanding* setting was that we used to place a new policy on the back of the toilet door. Staff informed us that this was a good way of reading the policies and even though this seemed odd, it worked!

Staff meetings were also another way of making sure that every member was kept up to date and also, the policies were signed by the staff to certify that they understood the new changes. This is also a good way of sharing good practice and ensuring that all staff members understand the changes and their implementation.

So contemplate, how do you make sure ALL staff members are aware of these changes if they do not attend staff meetings? Again, this is something that an inspector will ask the staff during the day of inspection.

Writing policies

It is an excellent idea to get your entire staff involved in writing your policies and serves as an additional mechanism to evaluate and embed your practice with current policies. This should not only include staff but also your committee members if you have a committee-run preschool.

During my time in Early Years, I have written more policies than I care to mention. I always dreaded the time when a new version or new legislation came into play, and I had to write yet another one adding to the vast 50 we had!

As time progressed, it became easier, with the use of a structured format. The list is immense and here are a few examples:

- Accident and Incident Policy
- Admissions Policy
- Behaviour Policy
- Biting Policy
- Compliment and Complaints Policy
- Equal Opportunities Policy
- Healthy Eating Policy
- Lost or Missing Child Policy
- Non-Collection of Child Policy
- Risk Assessment Policy
- Safeguarding Children Policy
- Settling-in Policy
- Trip Policy
- Whistleblowing Policy

These documents are very important as they will help you run your setting effectively and show the inspector you have a good understanding of your business operations. Again, make sure they are unique to your setting.

Training and qualifications

The inspector will want to check the details of the training attended by you and your staff and also the associated IMPACT (there is that word again!) it has had on your setting and the children.

We know training staff can be a problematic issue, particularly with lack of money, time out of the setting and finding the right course to meet the needs of staff members. You should be able to have documented records about the needs of your staff through the instated supervision and appraisal process. Their use can help you find the right course and at the time of inspection provide evidence that you are trying to upskill your workforce in order to make a difference within your setting.

The training stipulations also apply to the childminder and their assistants. As their manager, you need to show the inspector that you value each of your team as an employee and are actively encouraging new knowledge and skills in your setting.

The Statutory Framework for Early Years Foundation Stage (2017) states:

Staff qualifications, training, support and skills

3.21. 'The daily experience of children in Early Years settings and the overall quality of provision depends on all practitioners having appropriate qualifications, training, skills, knowledge, and a clear understanding of their roles and responsibilities.

Providers must ensure that all staff receive induction training to help them understand their roles and responsibilities. Induction training must include information about emergency evacuation procedures, safeguarding, child protection, and health and safety issues. Providers must support staff to undertake appropriate training and professional development opportunities to ensure they offer quality learning and development experiences for children that continually improves.

Childminders are accountable for the quality of the work of any assistants, and must be satisfied that assistants are competent in the areas of work they undertake.'

This reporting requirement and documentation is needed to demonstrate that your staff members are constantly improving on their skills.

The question that arises is: How do you do that?

Professional development questions

Part of the inspection process will pertain to assessing the impact training has had on your setting, staff and children.

Inspectors will want to see the staff's continuous professional development folder and ask the following questions:

- What was the last training that was attended, and what you did when you returned to the settings?
- Did you do anything with the new information you were given?
- Do staff members complete a training evaluation sheet and share with the rest of your staff?
- Do you share information at your staff meeting so that everyone who was unable to attend can get an insight into what was learned?

What is the point of this, I hear you say?

Firstly, think about how each staff member has their own learning journey, just like your children. You observe, assess, and plan for children. Here's something that must be carefully noted: Training is exactly the same for staff members.

- You observe staff in your setting on a day-to-day level.
- You assess where they are in their understanding.

- You plan to help them improve, and hence the new training.

Remember that training is not just a tick box exercise. You need to ensure knowledge enrichment and improvement, and this is not only through face-to-face training. Several other ways can be utilised to achieve knowledge development:

- Reading a book.
- E-learning.
- Reading blogs or journals.
- Attending other settings and sharing best practice.
- Attending conferences.

One thing which needs to be reiterated is that we also can improve upon our practice.

Think back to this: Do you ever get days where you observe your staff and think that they have lost their way a bit? They seem to have lost their mojo, which is impacting the delivery of children's learning?

Have you ever felt that way for yourself?

Ask yourself this: When was the last time you had **FIRE IN YOUR BELLY**?

Collins Dictionary states that *'If you say that someone has fire in their belly, you are expressing approval of them because they are energetic, enthusiastic, and have very strong feelings.'*

- When was the last time you had those feelings?
- What made you feel energetic and excited to share, learn and influence more?

- Do you still have those feelings? If not, why not?
- What do you feel you need to get it back again? Is it motivation? Is it time? Is it training?
- Or is it all of the above?

Training and continuous development is another non-negotiable reporting requirement. Inspectors need to explore how you are ensuring the staff's upskilling and consistent improvement.

The findings of the Nutbrown Review in 2012 helped with the understanding of how important upskilling and our continual professional development. It stated:

'Good quality CPD enables existing practitioners to build on their knowledge and skills and to keep up-to-date with relevant research, practices and initiatives, including learning from examples in other countries. Practitioners who undertake regular CPD show a proper respect for the children and families they work with, taking a professional pride in their work and demonstrating an understanding of their responsibility to constantly improve their practice and enhance the experience they are able to offer young children.'

This is extremely important in Early Years, our staff, parents, committee members, as well as our inspector, are continually told that we are a workforce that needs to be valued, nurtured, and trained.

One of the findings of the Nutbrown Review was that over half of the settings stated that the range and qualifications of the training did not meet the needs of their staff. Specifically, 72% identified that the cost of training and covering staff members attending the training put a huge strain on their financial status, which prevented the staff from attending this course.

Nutbrown (2012) emphasised the importance of accessing courses by the settings to grow their workforce and also stressed this should be evidenced during the Ofsted inspection.

Thinking back to the chapter on self-evaluation, remember:

WHAT

SO WHAT

NOW, WHAT?

What was the point of the training?

Are you able to demonstrate the evidence of the impact of training on you and your setting? If yes, how are you able to show this?

Qualifications

A couple of years ago, the Department for Education (2014) stated that staff who were level 3 qualified after 2014 needed to have Maths and English GCSE graded C or above to be included in the ratio. This guideline significantly impacted the number of Early Years educators who entered the workforce. College numbers decreased due to the only selective enrolment of students in the course based on their relevant GCSEs. The recruitment crisis was so overwhelming that it affected a major dent in the college classes and enrolment.

From April 2017, specific changes were incorporated in the new inspection framework. The changes were attributed to the consultation results stating that staff qualifying at level 3 Early Years Educator with any suitable English and Maths qualifications, in addition to functional skills as well as GCSEs should be included while computing the *staff: child* ratios. The Government's decision to reinstate functional skills is now encouraging recruitment in colleges as well as apprenticeships.

Your inspector will want to see copies of your staff's qualification and will record this as part of their evidence for your report.

Ratios

According to the EYFS (2021), for children aged below the age of two:

- There must be at least one member of staff for every three children.
- At least one member of staff must hold a full and relevant level 3 qualification and must be suitably experienced in working with children under two years of age (think how you can demonstrate this - training, past employment.
- At least half of all other staff must hold a full and relevant level 2 qualification.
- At least half of all staff must have received training that specifically addresses the care of babies.
- Specific to children under two-years-old, any member of staff assigned to their room must, as per the judgement of the provider, have suitable experience of working with children below the age of two.

This will need to be evidenced in the report that your inspector is writing while they are at your setting.

For children aged two:

- There must be at least one staff member for every four children.
- At least one staff member must hold a full and relevant level 3 qualification.
- At least half of all other staff members must hold a full and relevant level 2 qualification.

For children aged three and above, in registered Early Years provision where a person with Qualified Teacher Status, Early Years Professional Status, Early Years Teacher Status or another suitable level 6 qualification is working directly with the children:

- There must be at least one staff member for every thirteen children.
- At least one other staff member must hold a full and relevant level 3 qualification.

For children aged three and above at any time, in registered Early Years provision when a person with Qualified Teacher Status, Early Years Professional Status, Early Years Teacher Status or another suitable level 6 qualification is not working directly with the children:

- There must be at least one staff member for every eight children.
- At least one staff member must hold a full and relevant level 3 qualification.
- At least half of all other staff members must hold a full and relevant level 2 qualification.

Only staff members aged 17 or above may be included in the computation of the ratios. As such, it becomes necessary to know the following:

- Do you have volunteers in your setting?
- Do you know if you can include them in your ratios?

Students who are on long-term placements and volunteers (aged 17 or above) and apprentices (aged 16 or above) working towards a qualification may be included in the ratios as long as you are satisfied that they are competent and responsible.

You must be able to ensure that this guideline is adhered to while computing the ratios and appropriately demonstrated.

First aid

Much ambiguity seems to exist when it comes to First Aid and the use of such training in settings. This section will give you further clarity into the necessary requisites to ensure you meet the needs of the Statutory Framework.

To be compliant with Ofsted Statutory Framework for Early Years Foundation Stage (EYFS 2021) requirements, your staff should have a requisite number of members trained on First Aid from appropriate recognisable organisations, approved by HSE and Ofsted.

The training should cover the following:

1. Training needs to be designed for workers caring for young children in the absence of their parents and is appropriate for the age of the children being cared for.

2. Following training, an assessment of competence needs to lead to an award of a certificate.
3. This certificate must be renewed every three years.

With regard to the EYFS and Ofsted requirements, you should at least have one twelve-hour Full Paediatric First Aid qualified staff member available including medical cover for sickness, holidays, and trips. The twelve-hour Paediatric First Aid trained staff can be supported by One Day Emergency Paediatric First Aid trained staff.

This requirement must be revisited and renewed every three years. Ensure that if your staff members and children are going on trips, one staff member must be First Aid trained and carry a First Aid kit when they are out with the children. In addition, during any excursion, you will need to consider the number of children, staff, and layout of your setting to ensure that a Paediatric First Aider is able to respond to emergencies expeditiously.

All newly qualified staff to the Early Years workforce who have completed a level 2 and/or level 3 qualification on or after **30 June 2016,** MUST also have either a Full PFA or an Emergency PFA certificate within **three** months of commencing work in order to be included in the required staff: child ratios at level 2 or level 3 in an Early Years setting.

Your inspector will check this ratio on the day of the inspection and would want to see those certificates, which ideally should be on display or made available to parents if needed. Please be mindful that if you have these on display and in accordance with the GDPR regulations, you should have the necessary staff permission to display anything resulting in complete exposure of their names.

As evidenced in this chapter, training, and qualification is highly important to ensure that you are delivering high-quality learning to children and it has a positive and long-lasting IMPACT on their development. One thing to remember is to reflect on your learning process and think about how it is likely to impact your role as a teacher - today as well as in the future. While there is no one-size-fits-all recommendation, no matter where you are in your career or learning, these pointers will hold you in good stead and play a constructive role in helping you attain *outstanding*.

We have put together for you a training evaluation form which you can use when staff have attended training. Encourage them to complete this and share at the staff meeting.

www.jigsawearlyyearsconsultancy.com/are-you-ready-for-your-inspection-book-downloads/

The password is #AUR3-2022

Throughout the whole Leadership and Management chapter, you will have realised that evaluating your practice is of high priority. Ensure this approach is constant and integrated with the processes, as this constitutes a part of your own reflection of your setting as well as practice.

During the inspection process, you will also be expected to engage in a leadership and management discussion with the inspector. With this in mind, we have created a list of questions, which may help you ensure you are fully aware and completely prepared for this time:

1. How do you make sure the staff are gaining more knowledge and improving their skills?

2. How often do you conduct supervisions and appraisals?
3. How do the staff get involved with these processes?
4. What is the induction process for your staff?
5. What is your DBS process?
6. How do you cascade information to the staff?
7. What do you understand about Prevent Duty?
8. If I was to ask a member of staff about Prevent Duty would they know what it meant? (The inspector will also speak to a staff member).
9. If you had concerns who would you speak with?
10. What do your staff know about British Values and how are these incorporated and applied in the setting?
11. How do you ensure you are listening to staff regarding the workload and their well-being issues?
12. Who is the Lead Safeguarding officer?

Supporting staff wellbeing issues

This is an addition to the Education Inspection Framework (2019) and you will have to prove and maybe evidence how you consistently support your staff with their well-being issues. When delivering training for the new framework, this, in fact, emerged as the most debated topic. Providers, leaders, and managers have raised their eyebrows and sighed. The reason being, they feel that they listen to staff regarding their well-being and needs; and this is another tick box exercise. It is noted that when staff and the team are happy and contented within the setting, staff are more likely to perform better. Thereby, adding impact to children's lives and helping them achieve more success in the setting. Moreover, work-related stress has a huge impact on our own performance and our own well-being, as well as those with whom we are working, i.e. children.

This has become even more apparent since Covid-19.

Use this time to get you and your staff in the right mindset of being honest and map ideas on how you can improve on your well-being. Do this now. During your regular staff meeting ensure that each month you take ten minutes to focus on how you can improve this within your setting. This would then automatically reflect in your minutes and your inspector will be able to see this is raised at every opportunity to support the staff who needs it.

Now you may ask who is there to support you if you are the owner/leader or manager. Think about this for a minute or two and focus on when the last time you took a break - just for 30 minutes to give yourself some time to reboot. I know this is hard, as I always used to eat my lunch, if I had any, of course, at my desk while I was answering emails and writing on the computer.

This is not good for our minds or our well-being and I cannot stress enough about taking a break. Schedule one break in your diary and stick to that time for de-stressing yourself. Once you start doing this you will find your performance at work will become higher and more achievable as you will be able to focus on some breathable time.

We have created a mental well-being toolkit for you to download. Please visit the website.

www.jigsawearlyyearsconsultancy.com/are-you-ready-for-your-inspection-book-downloads/

The password is #AUR3-2022

10

SO NOW WHAT

So, you have taken the time to read the book, dived into each chapter to explore what you need to do to be prepared for your inspection. And, what do you do next?

I am hoping you will have made notes along the way as an 'Action Plan' of what you are planning to improve upon. This is an excellent way of reflecting on your practice, as well as showcasing your evaluation process to the inspector, as this is still a reporting requirement. I am hoping you can now see how important your INTENT, IMPLEMENTATION, AND IMPACT is on the day-to-day running of your setting.

Since our last edition of this book, we are delighted that our #JustQuality ADDING IMPACT accreditation is now seeing outstanding results and won a Nursery World award. It took us over six months to devise the programme, which not only helps you to evaluate where you are in your setting but also helps you to showcase the associated impact. It is all about IMPACT!

We have settings that are embarking on the #JustQuality journey and have been receiving amazing comments from inspectors. This is not to say that it is only the accreditation that has achieved these results. It is the staff's motivation and constant reflection on what they need to improve upon that has enabled them to achieve the most prestigious of grades.

There may still be times when you are thinking about what else can I do? I need an outsider to come in with a fresh pair of eyes to see it for themselves.

This is exactly where Jigsaw Early Years Consultancy Ltd can come to help you.

You have read the background and the WHY of us at the very beginning of this book. If this is something you feel you may benefit from then give us a ring, write to us, or feel free to drop in a message.

Our website is www.jigsawearlyyearsconsultancy.com

Our Facebook page is: www.facebook.com/JigsawEYC/

If you are an owner or manager reading this we have a bespoke group just for you!

Early Years Manager Impact group: www.facebook.com/groups/1480672328789426/

Facebook group: Are You Ready for Your Inspection

www.facebook.com/groups/320915655170338

11

TESTIMONIALS

I thought I would leave you with a few testimonials from settings that have used our Quality Improvement Inspections as part of their evaluation.

Dear Vanessa,

Thank you very much for your visit to our nursery for a Quality Improvement Inspection. As a twice 'Outstanding' nursery, who work incredibly hard to maintain that standard all of the time, we really wanted to be ready, to be confident and as well prepared for our big day as we could be to put us in the best possible position to maintain our grading, so felt that a QII would be exactly what we needed. You were recommended to us by a trusted colleague, and now we recommend you in turn.

Your visit was inspiring; you were professional and courteous, thorough and that filled us with confidence in your feedback. Staff were given valuable experience of inspection and were left feeling more confident, and even excited for their opportunity to shine. Your manager's interview and paperwork review were thorough and found a few issues that we have been able to rectify before they cost us our Outstanding, which was exactly what we wanted.

We have already booked you to come and give our new nursery a QII, as well as some consultancy on how to develop that new team, and I am excited and confident about our future, knowing that I have your input and support behind me and my team.

Thank you very very much again for such a positive experience.

With kindest regards,

Charlotte de Lacey, The de Lacey Montessori School & The de Lacey Day Nursery School.

So here's the update I promised!

Since the beginning of May, I have been waking up every morning thinking 'today's the day'. The six months from our inspection had passed. The changes needed to meet standards had been met or were being addressed. We were ready for a visit. I truly wanted it to happen before the summer holidays, so the team could have a well-earned rest.

Vanessa came back on Monday 2nd July 2018. She was blown away by the changes that had taken place. The setting was vibrant, energetic and full of happy children and staff. She agreed that we were ready for a visitor from HMI. There were 3 days left until the end-of-term. Surely they wouldn't come now?

Wednesday 3rd July... All the children were registered and had begun their last full day of planned learning. I looked at the clock, 9:35 am. I had lost hope that we'd be inspected before the summer break.

Then the Deputy Head popped her head into the room and looked at me with huge eyes, "Ofsted are here!" Behind me was a scene of devastation. The children had had a lot of fun that morning.

My TA and I looked at each other. Without saying a word to each other we knew what to do! Carry on and just do what we would normally do. I asked the children to put their wiggly fingers to work and tidy up. It was as if they could tell that they needed to do their best. Each child went off and completed a little task. One little boy looked at me and said, "We're doing a good job just for you". (A goose bump moment mixed with a slight feeling nausea).

As the inspector arrived in the Early Years block I was in the middle of my phonics session. The children were on form! We had laughing and the children knew all their first three sets of sounds.

Somehow during all of this I had managed to find the time to phone Vanessa. The inspector wanted to speak to her too!

I was asked to attend an interview at 12:30pm with the inspector. It was a grilling, but I survived with support from my Deputy and Head also present. I started waffling about my passion for the department. Then verbal diarrhoea kicked in! He wanted me to supply him with some pieces of evidence to back up my claims. I ran off and returned them to him. He was on his own in the office. He thanked me and said with a wry smile "I think what I'm seeing here is rather good".

At the end of the day the Head called us all together and said that although she was not legally able to divulge the outcome of the inspection she wanted us all to go home and have a well-earned rest with maybe a few glasses of bubbles.

Now the long wait over the summer holidays for the report and findings to be audited. Watch this space for the next update. Another HUGE thank you to Vanessa. We couldn't have got to this point without your help.

There really aren't enough stars available to show just how amazing Jigsaw Early years consultancy are.

The products are always of such a high quality and an invaluable tool within my setting. I have attended many training courses and all have left me feeling confident and reassured along with learning more and more every time.

The inspection academy was just outstanding and a lifeline for any manager.

The mastermind group has created a new amazing group of friends to support one another day in and day out.

The team at Jigsaw are so kind, welcoming and helpful armed with a wealth of knowledge. Vanessa has to be one of the most passionate, caring people I am yet to meet and inspires us daily in our practice.

To finish off if you have not attended EPOP then that is top of your to do list!!!!!!

Keep shining team Jigsaw you make Early years rock x

Ruth Hassey, Rivenstars

Vanessa and her team are absolutely wonderful. Vanessa's knowledge, experience and practicality is second to none. With Vanessa's help, at our latest inspection, we were awarded an Outstanding Ofsted grade - this was only possible because of Jigsaw Early Years Consultancy. Best money we have ever spent!

Roseanne Pool, Nursery on New Manor

Vanessa spent a full day at our nursery and I can honestly say it was the most interesting, beneficial experience we have ever had. Vanessa has to be one of the most knowledgeable and experienced professionals within the Early Years sector I have ever met. She simply oozes with passion and to quote Vanessa herself, she very definitely has 'fire in her belly' for everything Early Years.

We gained so much from Vanessa's visit, she gave us lots of useful pointers and ideas to enable us to further improve some areas of our practice. Most importantly for us though, she boosted our confidence in the work that we have been doing surrounding loose parts and evolving our learning environments to continue to inspire our children's natural curiosity.

Thank you so much, Vanessa, spending a day in your company was for all of us truly inspiring.

Jane Broughton, Manager of Tinkerbells Bridge inn Day Nursery, Preston, Lancashire

Finding #justquality was like finding the missing piece in our jigsaw (no pun intended). It epitomised everything I was looking for in an accreditation and has really helped us as a setting value the difference we make in children's lives and has really helped us drive our setting forward. It has helped the whole of my staff teams realise the WHY we do things and just how much impact even the smallest things have on our settings ethos, and more importantly our children, families and staff team!

Chloe Heath Edwards, Owner of 3 nurseries
Little Men and Misses Nursery

'I had been looking for a 'consultant' to come in and evaluate the performance of my staff and the environment of my setting. I felt that my staff were not performing as well as they have done in the past. I wanted to find a way of improving performance and practise overall and get the setting back on track to aim for OUTSTANDING. But it needed to be from someone who had 'authority' and for my staff to hear it from someone other than me.

I decided to sign up to the '#Just Quality ADDING IMPACT' award. It appealed to me as it's a journey for the whole setting to embark upon, to reflect on 'quality' and adding IMPACT - being a recognised accreditation was a Bonus.

However, before starting the accreditation, I felt it prudent to have an 'unannounced' Quality Improvement Inspection by Vanessa Dooley, Jigsaw Early Years Consultancy. Vanessa had been highly recommended to me by a fellow Day Nursery Owner who had also had a very effective QII from Vanessa and was also working towards the accreditation. Whilst there are other 'consultants' out there, I felt Vanessa's Ofsted Inspector training, knowledge, background & experience would be beneficial.

On 3rd July 2019 - Vanessa conducted an announced QII. Her findings (as detailed in the QII Report which she provides after inspecting) were shocking and disappointing - however, this was the 'wake up call' that was very much needed!!! I was actually pleased that Vanessa's was able to identify and highlight areas of underperformance and how our biggest resource, 'The Staff' were missing opportunities to provide quality teaching and learning opportunities to the children. Vanessa has an in-depth knowledge of Tapestry (which we use) and was, therefore, able to identify that our current 'tracking of children's progress' was ineffective. She conducted observations with my manager who was shocked by some of the staff's missed opportunities and immediately realised things needed to change too.

We held a staff training meeting with Vanessa at the end of the day (after the QII) to discuss the QII Report and to use this as a starting point for our '#JQAD' journey. We used the QII Report to put action plans in place to get back on track. The staff training/meeting was very positive and the team were buzzing with excitement to move forward together on improving quality and adding impact.

I cannot begin to tell you how incredibly amazing Vanessa is... She has truly transformed my setting. My manager and deputy have redistributed their roles and responsibilities to utilise their strengths and the manager is now going into each room daily to observe, model, guide and support staff. The Impact of the QII has been huge and worth every penny and more!!!

If you are needing someone to be brutally honest, highlight the positives, identify the weaknesses and get your team back on track, then Vanessa is the person you need! My only regret is that I didn't know about Vanessa sooner!

Jane Deighton, Owner - Little Faces Childcare

12

FINAL WORDS

Thank you for taking the time to read this book. I know there have been many of you who have contacted me to let me know what you think and I am truly honoured to read every one of them. If you do want to find out more about what we do and how I/we can help you with your inspection on adding impact then please get in touch my email is vanessa@jigsaweyc.com.

I did not intend to use this book as a tool to help promote Jigsaw Quality Improvement Audits but to help you in your upcoming Ofsted inspections, however, if you do wish us to visit and help you along the way... send us a message.

I often have said during the writing of this... *I wish I had this book when I was due an inspection!*

And, if you are saying the same, then my mission is complete.

I want you to shine in your inspection and showcase your setting. It is your one and only chance! And if I can help you with that at all I have succeeded in my mission!

Remember – It is all about IMPACT!

Printed in Great Britain
by Amazon